'Curtis Woodhouse is one of the most compelling and funniest sportsmen I have ever met. He brings the contrasting worlds of professional football and boxing to life – in a way that is as brutally honest as it is gripping, amusing and illuminating. Woodhouse, in the company of his skilled co-writer Ben Dirs, has produced a riveting read. If you're interested in football, boxing or, most of all, real life, *Box to Box* will draw you in and keep you hooked.' Donald McRae, *The Guardian*, author of *Dark Trade, In Black & White* and *A Man's World* and twice winner of the Willam Hill Sports Book of the Year award.

BOX TO BOX

From the Premier League to British Boxing Champion

Curtis Woodhouse

with Ben Dirs

**SIMON &
SCHUSTER**

London · New York · Sydney · Toronto · New Delhi

A CBS COMPANY

First published in Great Britain by Simon & Schuster UK Ltd, 2016
A CBS COMPANY

1 3 5 7 9 10 8 6 4 2

Simon & Schuster UK Ltd
1st Floor
222 Gray's Inn Road
London WC1X 8HB

www.simonandschuster.co.uk
www.simonandschuster.au
www.simonandschuster.co.in

Simon & Schuster Australia, Sydney
Simon & Schuster India, New Delhi

The author and publishers have made all reasonable efforts to contact
copyright-holders for permission, and apologise for any omissions or errors in
the form of credits given. Corrections may be made to future printings.

A CIP catalogue record for this book
is available from the British Library.

ISBN: 978-1-4711-4772-2
eBook ISBN: 978-1-4711-4774-6

Typeset and designed in the UK by M Rules
Printed in the UK by CPI Group (UK) Ltd, Croydon, CR0 4YY

CONTENTS

COULDA BEEN A CONTENDER

Hull, autumn 2005

When I was a kid, I thought my dad was a superhero. I used to say to him: 'Dad, where will you go when you die?' And he'd say to me: 'I'll never die, son. Dying's for everyone else. I'm a superhero.' So when I say I thought my dad was a superhero, I really did. I believed him. I thought he'd live forever.

When Dad wasn't being a superhero – or lugging bricks or laying kerbs or digging holes – he ran a pub called The Clarendon, just round the corner from the KC Stadium. When I signed for Hull City in 2005, The Clarendon became my local. For a few months at least. Finish training at 12.30, on the Guinness by 1.00. I grew up down the road in Driffield, so playing for Hull was the dream. Or so people thought, from the outside looking in: 'Look at him – professional footballer, playing for his local team! Big house, fast car, loose women! Lucky bastard.'

Truth was, I'd rather have been anywhere else. I hated every minute of being at Hull City and I hated what football had done to me. Time was up, I couldn't carry on. But how do you tell your superhero dad that you've pissed it all away, ripped up the golden ticket, didn't even have the decency to train and not get drunk? But Dad wasn't daft. He'd seen almost every game I'd played, from when I was a kid. He'd borrowed plenty of tenners, money he couldn't afford to pay back, just so he could fill up the car and drive me to training, games and trials the length and breadth of the country. So much time and effort invested. And for what? But he knew better than anyone that I wasn't really there, was just going through the motions. Then came the phone call: 'What are you up to today?'

'Nowt. Just finished training.'

'Fancy a couple of beers?'

I never needed my arm twisting. So there I was, finished training at 12.30, on the Guinness by 1.00.

'We'll stay here all day, shall we?'

'Yeah, can do. I'm not doing owt.'

So, after a couple of pints I told him.

'Listen, Dad, I'm done with football. This is my last season. I'm gone. I've had enough.'

I was upset, confused. People don't retire from being a professional footballer at 25. I must be doing something wrong?

'What are you gonna do?' said Dad. 'Come and work with me, digging holes from six in the morning to five at night?'

Dad had dug so many holes he was riddled with arthritis in his knees and elbows.

'I make £300 a week for digging holes, you're on thousands of pounds a week and you train from 10.30 to 12.30. You need to sort yourself out, son.'

'Dad, I'm gonna become a professional boxer. I don't know what else to do.'

Afternoon turned into evening and there were Hull City fans coming in and out all day.

'Ah, there's Curtis Woodhouse, let me buy you a drink . . .'

I'd never met so many blokes who coulda been a contender that day. Blokes telling stories about trials they'd had for Hull City, trials they'd had for Sheffield United, trials they'd had for Hull Kingston Rovers. Everyone I spoke to seemed to have had trials for some team or other in Yorkshire, whether it was football, rugby league or cricket. Half of them got offered contracts but none of them ever signed one, because something always happened to crush the dream. They discovered women, they discovered booze, they'd 'done' their knee. That's always a favourite with the ones who never made it, the old 'done' knee. Nobody ever holds their hands up and says they simply weren't good enough or didn't make the most of their opportunity. And when you're the landlord of a pub, you hear these stories on repeat. Punters propping up the bar and getting better and better with every pint they sink.

Evening turned into night and the punters started drifting away.

'Top man, Curtis, good luck on Saturday. Score a goal for me . . .'

And in the end it was just me and Dad, plenty of pints in, pretty steaming.

'Son, you saw what happened here today? All these people coming up to you and talking shit about why they never got their shot?'

'I know. It's embarrassing, Dad. If one more person had told me about their dodgy knee . . .'

'You know what would be even more embarrassing? You know what would break my heart? If my own son was sat here in 10 years' time, one of those sad blokes propping up the bar and telling everyone he could have been a boxer. Fuckin' hell, I'd be so embarrassed I'd have to walk away from you.

'Son, I'm bored of hearing those stories. If you want to do it, go and do it. If you're not, never mention it again. Otherwise, you're just like that lot.'

CHAPTER 1

SMACK 'EM HARD

Driffield, when Liverpool ruled

There has probably been nobody else on earth, before or since, who loved football as much as I did. From the age of six, I'd wake up at seven in the morning and call on my Auntie Mandy, who lived in the next-door terrace. Sometimes she'd hand me a video of *Rocky IV* through the window, as if it was a drug transaction, and I'd run home and watch it. But usually I'd just stick a football under my arm, grab a packet of crisps from the kitchen and that was me for the day. I never really watched much TV or wanted any pets. Mum once offered to buy me one and I said I wanted a giraffe. My punishment for being naughty was being kept indoors, so I wasn't naughty very often. I just wanted to play football; it was pretty much the only thing that mattered in my life.

If it was a school day, I'd run home, wolf down dinner

and stay out playing football until it was so dark I couldn't see my hand in front of my face. All the kids on the estate used to join in, either on Northfield Crescent itself or on the car park round the back. One day the council put up a sign saying: 'NO BALL GAMES'. The next day, Dad came out with his screwdriver, tore it down and chucked it in a skip. Dad also welded a goal together and we'd play Wembley, where one person is in goal and it's everybody against everybody. It was brutal. The older kids used to call me names and try to kick lumps out of me. But even when I was tiny, I was one of the best. They couldn't get near me. And while I was dribbling past everyone, I'd be commentating in my head:

'Barnes . . . still Barnes . . . BARNES SCORES AGAIN!'

Because Liverpool were winning everything, I was a massive supporter and idolised John Barnes. Me and John Barnes were both left-footed, both good dribblers and, from when I was seven or eight years old to 17, he was all I ever wanted to be. Another reason I loved John Barnes was because he had the same colour skin as me. Even when he had bananas thrown at him, it didn't seem to affect him. And when you get picked on a lot, you need someone to look up to. Those games on Northfield Crescent were my football apprenticeship before my actual football apprenticeship. The one way I could say 'fuck you' was by winning. They could boot me or call me anything they wanted, but they had to accept I was better than them. On Northfield Crescent, as at Anfield, Barnes ran the show.

Driffield is a small market town in the East Riding of Yorkshire. There's not much going on in Driffield. Quiet, that's what I remember about it. Everyone knows everyone and everyone knows everyone else's business. But the people are salt of the earth, there's very little crime and it's somewhere I wouldn't mind my kids growing up. Mum is from Driffield and when I was growing up there were Armstrongs everywhere. About 10 of our family lived on Northfield Crescent and there were even more on Star Hill, the other estate down the road. Us kids were all really close because we were all about the same age. In the summer of 1979, Mum and Dad went on holiday to Butlin's with Auntie Jackie and Uncle Tony, and the following April me and my cousin Richard were born within two days of each other. That was obviously some trip.

About 20 of us used to walk home from school together and get dropped off in bunches. They were more innocent times in many ways. Talking about those days now, it almost sounds like I'm describing the 1960s. Sometimes I'd come home with a handful of pennies and Mum would ask me where I got them from. I'd say: 'The Penny Man gave them to me to buy an ice cream.' When this became a bit regular, Mum got alarmed and took it upon herself to find out who this Penny Man was. It turned out he was a lovely old fella called Cockney George, who used to fix tellies and was drunk most days. He had a bike but you never saw him ride it – it was just to keep him upright. Because everybody is so paranoid nowadays, nobody plays on the streets anymore. Never mind the Penny Man, a drop of rain and Mummy and Daddy start shitting themselves. But we used to disappear all day, with no questions asked. I was outside so often I barely knew my mum. It would be school, football, home for tea, bath and bed. And the same the next day.

It sounds like a perfect childhood, but life wasn't always easy. Mum was white as snow and Dad was black as the ace of spades, so from an early age I was aware I was different. The only people in Driffield who were the same colour as me were my little brother Karl and sister Laura, Dad, his brother Carson and his two kids, Georgina and Kerry, and Auntie Mandy. Other than that, there were no black people for about 50 miles, or at least it seemed that way.

We used to get called 'nigger' all the time. Or 'nignog'. Or 'gollywog'. Or 'Paki'. I reckon me, my brother and my sister used to get called something horrible at least 20 times a day. In school, out of school, pretty much every-where we went. One birthday, I handed out invitations and got one reply back saying: 'My son won't be coming to your party because you're a nigger.' Mum would be walk-ing me in a pram and women would peer in and say: 'Ooh, has Mummy been perming your hair?' Or: 'Has Mummy taken you away on holiday?' Mum would be stood there, so white she was almost translucent. My next-door neighbour but one even had a black Labrador called Nigger. Me and my brother would be out playing football and we'd hear her shouting:

'Come on, Nigger, time for dinner!'

We'd look at each other and say: 'Is she talking to me, you or the dog?'

She was a lovely lady with a lovely family but that was the world we lived in. She probably didn't even realise it was offensive.

When we played football, there was no escape either. Whereas I thought I was John Barnes, other kids preferred to think of me as nigger . . .

'Barnes down the left wing . . .'

'Fuck you, nigger . . .'

'Barnes cuts inside . . .'

'Fuck you, nigger . . .'

'Barnes with an effort from long range . . .'

'Fuck you, nigger . . .'

'BARNES!'

'FUCKING NIGGER!'

That lot from Northfield Crescent, they're all my friends now. They always were. They were just uneducated. I wasn't much better – I used to call the newsagent's round the corner 'Tony's Paki Shop'. I didn't even know what the word nigger meant when I was small. I don't think half of them did either. That's why I don't think badly of the people who said it. But I knew it wasn't a nice word because people weren't smiling when they spat it out. It used to really upset me. As a kid, I'd feel like I'd done something wrong. But it used to upset Dad more than it did us, because he understood the significance. And when he explained to us what nigger meant, that upset me even more. Ignorance is bliss.

When people started calling me names and threatening to beat me up, usually after I'd scored another goal and made them look silly, I'd run down the cut next to my house as fast as my little legs would carry me – it was only about 10 yards but it felt like miles – go flying through the door and lock it behind me. If Mum and Dad weren't home, I'd open the front window, stick my head out and start giving them stick: 'I beat you again! You're all shit!' But sometimes, Dad would be waiting for me and give me the lecture:

'Listen, do you want to be running for the rest of your life? It's embarrassing, son. Get out there and fight. From now on, if anyone ever calls you nigger, smack 'em as hard as you can, straight in the face. Do that every time someone calls you nigger and after a while they'll stop calling you it.'

At first, I didn't want to do it because I'd be thinking: 'This kid is way bigger than me; if I hit him I'm going to get filled in.' Dad would still have to do my dirty work for me. He'd storm out of the house and start shouting and waving his fist. 'If any of you bastards calls my son that again, they'll have me to deal with!' But I soon got a taste for it. Eventually they realised that they didn't really enjoy fighting and that if they called me or my brother that name, I was going to smack 'em. I wasn't going to win – I was one of the worst fighters ever – but in the end they'd think: 'I can't be arsed. Let's go and pick on someone with a bit less about them.' That was my amateur boxing career, on North-field Crescent: 50-odd fights, not a single win but plenty of seasoning.

Without Nana there is no me and I wouldn't be telling this story. Dad and Uncle Carson were twins, born in 1956. Their mum, Nana Bess, was from Jamaica. I'm not sure if she brought Dad and Uncle Carson to England or got pregnant over here, but when she went back she left them behind. Dad's actual name isn't Bernard, it's Barnardo, because that's what they called him after they were dumped in Barnardo's children's home. I don't know too much about his family background, it's not something he ever spoke about, but I do know Nana went down to London, adopted both of them and gave Dad his new name. She was in an abusive relationship at the time – her husband used to beat her up – so she had to give them back to Barnardo's until she could leave this fella. Twelve months later, she took them back again.

To take them in once was amazing; to take them in twice was almost unbelievable. This was Bridlington, Yorkshire, in the 1950s. She'd get called all the names under the sun, have stuff thrown through her windows, shoved through her letterbox, and be spat at in the street. Imagine that, pushing two toddlers in a pram and people are spitting at you. They should have been lining the streets and applauding. It was an incredible thing to do and she was an incredible woman. She adopted Auntie Mandy as well, who is also black but not blood related to Dad and Uncle Carson. The man I knew as Grandpa was Walter. Walter lived with Nana until the day he died, so all three children were very fortunate to end up in such a stable environment.

Nana was very stubborn and very strict. She didn't take any shit. Every Sunday we'd go round for dinner and she'd boss Dad around: 'Stop doing this, Bernard, do this, Bernard, put that back, Bernard . . .' He'd be running around like a blue-arsed fly. Dad was an alpha male; I never heard anyone else tell him what to do, so to see him getting bullied by Nana used to make us giggle. Meanwhile, when Nana Bess came to visit from Jamaica, she would be sitting in our house, not 10 yards away. Uncle Carson lived 100 yards down the street and never spoke to her. Even as a young kid I thought that was weird. Then again, Nana Bess didn't really speak to anybody. When I picture her, she's hitting me with her red slipper.

Mum and Dad met in a pub in Driffield. At the time, the pubs in Driffield were only open Thursday to Sunday. So every weekend would end up like the OK Corral. We used to get all these squaddies over from the army barracks in Beverley, which is where I was actually born, and this one night it all went off and there were about 30 people going at it, throwing punches from all angles and swinging chairs around their heads. After it all died down, Dad was stood at the bar with this big black eye and Mum said to him: 'Oooh, you all right, love?' And he said: 'Course I am, you stupid cow.' That was the first time they spoke to each other. A week later he was out with his mates and Mum was in the pub again. One of Dad's mates said to him: 'Dare you to go and speak to that bird over there with the big tits.' The rest is history.

Dad used to do any kind of manual labour during the week and work on the doors in Driffield of a weekend. Mum would soak his shirts in the bath and there would be blood everywhere. In the morning we'd ask what had happened and he'd regale us with all these gory war stories while we were having breakfast. Mum used to work in a place called Twydales, killing turkeys. I can never remember either Mum or Dad being out of work; they always worked a minimum of one job, sometimes two or three, to get us through. It's healthy for kids to see that; it's why I've always seen that level of graft as normal.

When Dad was growing up, he didn't have the luxury of picking and choosing whether he wanted to fight. The only person looking out for Dad, and vice versa, was his brother. If one was fighting, they were both fighting. There are only so many times you can be spat at in the street before you smack 'em as hard as you can. Dad used to say to me: 'You are either a lion or you are an antelope. And you know what happens to antelopes, son? They get fucked.'

Mum swam for Hull Olympic as a kid and was a decent long-distance runner, so that's where the sporty genes came from. Dad played a little bit of football locally, although if you listened to him you'd think he was on a par with Pele and Maradona. But he was in a bad car crash, broke both his legs and was in hospital for eight months. So that was his football career finished. But Dad's real love was boxing. He used to gather round the radio with his mates and listen to Mike Tyson fights. Dad was a big Joe Louis fan, but this kid Tyson would have beaten Joe Louis. This kid would have beaten anybody. But because Dad also liked Tyson, he was my first boxing hero. Although the funny thing was, for ages I thought Tyson was white. I guess that's how it goes, when you think of the colour of your skin as a negative.

My first victory was before my first lesson on my first day at secondary school, when I beat up a couple of twins. I couldn't tell them apart, so I hit both of them to make sure. I still speak to them now, they drink in Mum's pub in Driffield. I wasn't a saint at school by any stretch of the imagination, but I wasn't a horrible kid either. At least until

I stopped going completely. I'd do a lot of skiving but I was never rude to teachers, never cheeky. It wasn't in my nature; I was a nice kid really – there would never be any mums knocking on our door complaining about me. But you've got to stand up for yourself. If anyone wanted to abuse me, I'd smack 'em as hard as I could, straight in the face. Just like Dad taught me. You've got to take care of business. The other option was to do nothing and get bullied for the rest of my life.

While I was a big boxing fan and had plenty of scraps on the cobbles, the closest I got to boxing were punch-ups in Bobby Brooksby's front garden. I was about 10; he was about 16 and had four or five brothers. We'd wear cricket gloves, one glove each. I was small but I was willing. And I always got the first punch in, cricket glove or not. The only boxing gym I ever went to as a kid was Bridlington Boys' Club, when I was 12 and my brother Karl was 10. I sparred a kid in there and beat the granny out of him. Turned out the kid had had 30 fights. The trainer asked me what gym I'd come from and I said I'd come from Northfield Crescent. He couldn't believe I hadn't boxed before. To be honest, I still can't box now. But all that seasoning on Northfield Crescent meant I could always fight. The fact that this kid had had 30 fights didn't bother me; I just wanted to get in the ring and beat him up.

But I didn't enter another boxing gym for about seven years after that. Football was still my obsession.

CHAPTER 2

THE GOOD, THE BAD
AND THE UGLY

Birmingham, autumn 2003

E ver been trapped in a loveless relationship? One day you're head over heels and all set to take on the world together; a few years later it's all gone to shit. You've fallen out of love and you don't know how it happened. The dream has gone and it's impossible to get it back. Love and hate are similar emotions. And I really hated football. I'd hated football for years. I know, I know, poor me ...

How could I not love the game that every young boy wanted to play? What was wrong with me? But I knew I wasn't alone. The more people you talk to in football, the more you realise that lots of them don't like playing it. I reckon as many as one in three professional players dislikes the game. It's one of football's dirty secrets. Sounds crazy, I know. And I did feel guilty. But I'd given everything to the game since I was that skinny little kid on Northfield Crescent. And at some point it started being a job. And when that happened, everything changed. You're not playing for fun anymore; you're playing for a club, a manager, your wages, your bonuses. That skinny little kid running rings round the other kids on Northfield Crescent, getting called a nigger and wanting to prove everyone wrong – 'FUCK EVERYONE!' – he was dead and buried. The dream of being another John Barnes had long gone. Right, pack your bags, new club, new town, no plan, no direction, no ambition, no more than a pawn.

When Barry Fry rang me to ask if I wanted to join Peterborough, I had absolutely no interest.

'Curtis? Barry Fry. You wanna come and play for me at Peterborough?'

'No.'

'Why not?'

'One, because I don't even know where Peterborough is. Two, because I do know they're shit. Three, because I never want to play football again.'

'Listen, I understand what you're going through. But while you work out what you wanna do next, come and train with us, just to keep yourself fit.'

If I couldn't get myself up for playing for Birmingham in the Premier League, what chance did I have playing for that nutter in the Second Division? After a soul-destroying loan spell at Rotherham, I'd been out of the game for six months, getting pissed. And I still had a load of money – it wasn't as if I was running out any time soon. In my head, I was already a former footballer.

But I knew what Baz was up to: 'If I get him down here, he might enjoy it and end up signing.' And he was right, the crafty bastard. Once I started training, I got a new lease of life. Turned out I'd missed it. Football was my trade, what I excelled at, and I knew the game inside and out. I was always a footballer deep down; football was at my core, even when I despised it.

Having dropped down two divisions I found it easy, despite all the boozing and partying I'd done in Birmingham. Players in the lower divisions are technically good, but when you've been training with top players for so long your brain is sharper. You're always a step ahead; you see things developing that other players miss. It almost felt like I was cheating. So Baz made me skipper and in my first season at the club I won player of the year. Peterborough fans still tell me I kept them up that season. Baz called me 'Captain Marvel'. He'd say: 'He scores goals at one end and clears them off the line at the other.'

Because I was back on form, lots of clubs came in for me. Peter Taylor, who was my England Under-21s manager, wanted to take me to Hull City. But Baz was asking for crazy amounts. All that stuff about me being Captain Marvel was to bolster my confidence and make me play well for the team, but it was also him polishing up his investment, making it shinier so that he could sell it on for more money. I get it now – football is a business and the club was struggling financially. But I was a 24-year-old kid and just felt betrayed.

I came back the following season with the raving hump. I was on edge, aggressive. 'OK, you've seen the good, now you'll see the bad and the ugly.' Playing for Peterborough in front of a few thousand people was never part of the dream. So before you knew it I was boozing heavily again, causing mayhem, verbally and physically abusing everyone. The sort of things you do when a passion is dying and a relationship is spiralling out of control.

When we played Bristol City, I went for Bobby Gould in the dressing room at half-time. Bobby was Baz's head coach and I hated him. His philosophy on football was boot it as far as you possibly can. And that meant booting it over my head, which was no good for me. I'm not at Peterborough United for the benefit of the team; I'm at Peterborough United for the benefit of Curtis Woodhouse. If I want to move on from this shambles of a football club, I've got to play well. And to play well, I need my team-mates to pass me the ball every now and again: 'Give the ball to me – I'll take care of the rest!' Instead, I'm running around like an idiot in midfield. Bobby Gould managed the Crazy Gang at Wimbledon, so he was quite confrontational himself. Having him in charge was like pouring petrol on a blazing fire. This was a bloke who had won the FA Cup, was a respected manager and was getting on a bit, and my team-mates were having to drag me off him. I really wanted to kill him. He walked out, at half-time, and never came back. He was only trying to do what was best for the club. Embarrassing, really. If I saw him now, I'd apologise and try to explain what I was going through.

One day after training, Baz brought me into his office and said: 'Why are you so angry?! Every day in training, everyone is on eggshells.'

'I don't know, Barry. It's just how I am. It's my personality.'

But it wasn't my personality. I knew, deep down, that I was actually a nice kid. Baz didn't really know what to do with me. I was his best player by miles but causing all kinds of problems. Leon McKenzie was also at Peterborough and he came from boxing royalty. His uncle, Duke, won world titles at three different weights and his dad, Clinton, was a British and European champion. So all we used to do was talk boxing – before training, after training and even during training. So, eventually, Baz brought me in again.

'Listen, we can't carry on like this, it's a bloody nightmare for everyone. I know you love your boxing. There's a guy called Gary De'Roux who's got a gym round the corner from me. Why not go down there, hit the bag and knock off a bit of steam? Better than coming in and fighting people in training.'

People look at Baz and think he's this manager who rants and raves and throws cups around the dressing room. And they'd be right. But I've got a soft spot for him. He's all bark and no bite, a nice guy behind all that smoke, mirrors and bravado. He's a meat-and-two-veg kind of bloke – if he thinks you're a wanker, he'll call you a wanker. Even if he doesn't think you're a wanker, he'll call you a wanker. But at least he was trying to help me, and I was smashing up his football club. I could have done with that kind of intervention earlier. You could argue that I owe my boxing career to Barry Fry. Just don't tell him that – I'd never hear the last of it.

CHAPTER 3

LOVE AT FIRST SIGHT

Driffield, 1989

The first game I played for my school team might have been the only one Dad missed. But Howard Leech's dad was watching that day. Des Leech was a mate of Dad's and that night he paid us a visit.

'Have you seen your lad play football?'

'Yeah, I've seen him kicking it about outside the house. He's good.'

'Good? He's brilliant!'

I didn't know if I was good, bad or average – I was just playing for the love of the game. But when Dad came to see me play for the first time, he saw what Des Leech had seen and signed me up for Bridlington Rangers Under-10s. Playing for them wasn't much different from the kickabouts on Northfield Crescent: I'd get the ball, dribble past everyone and score. Just like Barnes.

At secondary school, I met a kid called Lee Morris. He was also a very good footballer, so we instantly clicked and became best mates. Lee, who I also played with for Bridlington, was the quickest white kid I ever saw and he had a wand of a left foot. One Saturday I went for a kickabout with Lee and his dad, Colin. Colin would run down the wing and cross it in, and we'd try to get on the end of it. That night I went home and said to Dad:

'You want to see Lee Morris's dad, he's unbelievable at football.'

'Yeah, I know, he used to play for Sheffield United.'

It turned out Colin Morris played more than 200 games for United and was a bit of a club legend. When me and Lee turned 14, and were still in York City's youth programme, Colin phoned up Sheffield United and asked if the two of us could come for a trial. We both signed a week later. We were at York together, went through Sheffield United's academy together, played for England together and made our first-team debuts within weeks of each other. Not bad for two classmates from a little Yorkshire town called Driffield.

I don't recall Dad ever telling me he loved me or giving me a hug. He was a hard, stubborn old man. My missus calls me an emotional retard, but Dad made me look slushy. He never told me how well I played or how good I might be. Instead it was, 'How on earth did you miss that?' or 'What the bloody hell were you up to there?' I'm not very good at accepting compliments anyway. And saying all that gooey stuff means very little – it's all about your actions. If Dad had no money in his pockets and I needed to go to a trial, he'd beg, steal or borrow to get me to wherever I needed to be, even if he had nothing to eat. They're some of my best memories as a kid, sitting next to Dad in his red Cortina with the black roof. We went all over the country in that thing. He'd have a Stevie Wonder tape on the stereo, or Ray Charles. Our favourite song was 'Hit the Road, Jack', which kind of made sense. The best part about football was the journey there and the journey back. Dad telling bloody war stories about his time working on the doors in Driffield, the fights he'd had, the blokes he'd beaten up, the women he'd met, the beer he'd drunk. He didn't spare me any details, even though I was only 12. I was a man before I became a teenager.

I had trials with just about every decent club up north, including Man United and Newcastle. If I'd told Dad I had a trial in Timbuktu he would have driven me all the way there. We went backwards and forwards to Man City for a couple of years, when Peter Reid was in charge. Dad's favourite player was Colin Bell, so when City sent me a letter asking me to come for a trial, Dad said: 'You're going there, son.' They really looked after us. But City's training ground used to be in Moss Side, which was seriously rough in the early 1990s. One night they put us up in this hotel, and I remember Dad sat there like he was some kind of king, tucking into this giant prawn cocktail, sipping a pint of John Smith's Smooth and saying: 'This is the life, son.' The next day we got up to go to the trial and his Cortina had been smashed up and the radio lifted.

About the only club I didn't go to was Leeds, which was strange given Dad was a big fan. When Mum and Dad first met, he took her to a Leeds game and halfway through the first half she got up to walk out.

'I'm not listening to this, Bernard, everyone singing, "Who's the bastard in the black?".'

'It's not me they're singing it to, you silly cow, it's the referee ...'

But as soon as I went to Sheffield United, I was hooked. It was like when you fall in love with a woman and some people are thinking: 'I can't work out what he sees in her.' She might not be the best looking, she might not have the best figure, she might be a bit on the large side, but the personality fits. Everyone was just so welcoming. I went along with Lee Morris, and Rob Strickland, who was from Hull, was also there. All three of us had played in the county team together so that made it easier to fit in. Newcastle offered me a two-year deal but I didn't want to go anywhere else. Me and Sheffield United was love at first sight.

Sat at the top of the stairs, petrified. A coin spinning in my head: 'Will it be peace and quiet tonight or 20 bulls running through the house?' I still get a tight chest thinking about it. At the time, I'd have a tight chest from Wednesday onwards. A state of panic. Most kids can't wait for the weekend. I was the opposite. During the week, our house was like *The Waltons*. Of a weekend, it could be carnage. I used to dread it.

... Sat at the top of the stairs, clutching my knees and waiting to cry, heart coming through my chest ... distant rough and tumble ... fumbling outside ... key finally in the door ... we're off the hook tonight ... slink off to bed, wait for the panic to subside and finally get some sleep ...

... Sat at the top of the stairs, clutching my knees and waiting to cry, heart coming through my chest ... distant rough and tumble ... fumbling outside ... key finally in the door ... no such luck tonight ... windows smashing, tables crashing, crockery bouncing off walls ...

It reached a point when anything less than murder was a bonus. 'Please, Dad, don't kill her ... please, Mum, don't die ...' Another stormy night on Northfield Crescent. Nights that shaped my life.

Between the ages of 10 and 14, I lived in a war zone. Northfield Crescent was my own little Beirut. I wouldn't wish those years on my worst enemy. On Sundays I'd escape with Dad to football or he'd take me, Karl and Laura to Bridlington to play in the arcades. And then Wednesday would roll round and the tight chest would kick in again, as if somebody had reached inside me, taken a grip and started twisting. Tick, tick, tick ... waiting for the bomb to go off. Then one day I woke up and everyone had gone.

'Morning, son. Your mum's not here anymore.'

I thought Dad meant she was dead.

'Where's she gone?'

'Moved away with your brother and sister.'

'Oh, right ...'

They'd all fucked off to Selby. Nobody had asked me. I think Mum just assumed I'd want to stay. I was Dad's eldest and we had a special bond. But it would have been nice to have been given the choice. Me and Dad stayed in the house until it got repossessed, and we were forced to move. Because Dad had no money, he'd be away working in London Monday to Friday, leaving me in the new house on my own at the age of 14. I'd bum about with Kevin Edgar, who lived next door but one, drinking cider and shooting birds with a pellet gun when we should have been at school. Then when Dad got home, he'd be so upset about losing Mum he'd cause mayhem.

When they got divorced, things became even worse. After a year or so, Mum and my brother and sister moved back to Driffield. Whenever Dad bumped into her, it ended in violence. So Mum hit him with an injunction. When he got charged with breaching it, people told me he'd go to jail. So I stood up in court at the age of 15 and committed perjury: 'It was dark, it was difficult to see. It wasn't my dad, it was me.' So Dad got off and the mayhem continued.

I hated Mum for leaving me in that war zone and it took me years to forgive her. I just couldn't understand why she never asked me to go with her. If someone had rung me and said, 'Your mum is dead', I wouldn't have cared. I blamed her for what the break-up had done to Dad. He'd been abandoned by his mum, so having his own family torn apart killed him. And when you see your superhero fall apart, you end up blaming someone. The obvious person was Mum. But as I got older, I started to see things differently. I realised Mum's life wasn't a bed of roses, either. Dad was my superhero, but he was no saint.

CHAPTER 4

GAZ AND BAZ

Peterborough, winter 2004

Sometimes you meet 'The One' when you're not even looking. Sometimes you might still be in a relationship. And when you do, you wonder why you've been flogging that dead horse for so long. While my football dreams had died, I knew I could still achieve something great. But it could have been in anything. Horse racing, mountain climbing, whatever. I was always a boxing fan, but I'd never actually boxed. If Baz had arranged a game of darts with Phil Taylor, I might have given that a go. If he'd sent me to see a ballet instructor, I might have become a ballerina. I was that lost. Luckily for my street cred, he sent me to a boxing gym. And suddenly I was smitten again. I was boxing for the reason I first played football – because I loved it. I was still only 24 and should have been enjoying life, but football wasn't doing it for me. So it was a feeling of youthful excitement combined with relief. And in Gary De'Roux I couldn't have had a better introduction to the not-so-noble art.

I knocked on Gary's door and this little black guy answered. I thought he was going to be huge. I knew he was a former British champion, but I didn't know he was a featherweight.

'Gary?'

'You must be Curtis. The footballer?'

'That's me.'

We shook hands, went round to his back garden and within minutes of me arriving on his doorstep Gary was taking me through the basics.

I liked Gaz instantly. He reminded me so much of Dad. He didn't say much and was very wary of everyone and everything: 'Why is he here? What's he come to look at? What's his angle?' But I needed a mentor at the time. For most of my football career I did whatever I wanted and went wherever I wanted, so it was good to have someone to rely on and be in charge of me. There were a lot of people dependent on me being a footballer, bringing money in, doling it out. A tenner here, 20 quid there, 50 quid here, 100 quid there. 'Can you lend me a grand for my car insurance? Have you got a couple of grand so I can sort my guttering? You're loaded, can't you get the drinks in?' Sometimes I'd feel like saying: 'But it's not my round!' People would come out with no money and expect me to buy drinks all night. If I didn't buy drinks all night, people would call me a wanker behind my back. If I did buy drinks all night, people would say: 'Who does he think he is, chucking his money about?'

Gaz was interested in me, and that made a change from

football. I used to sit down with him and his wife Linda after training and we'd talk about anything: 'How are the missus and the kids? Where are you living?' General chit-chat, rarely boxing. The best boxing trainers double as agony aunts, because nine times out of 10 they're dealing with kids who aren't from stable backgrounds. Gaz understood that there was something different about men who fight for a living. And it was nice to have a bit of interaction. Better than sitting in the bookies, spunking a load of dough on the horses. Without Gaz and Linda, my boxing career would never have got off the ground. They gave me that nurturing environment, the belief and the bare basics of how to box.

In the early days I was doing two or three sessions a week, and I'm talking about the raw fundamentals. I went down Brendan Ingle's gym a few times when I was at Sheffield United but that was just to beat the shit out of the heavy bag. So Gaz was teaching me footwork, how to throw a punch, basic combinations. As the football season went on, I started going every day. Learning new things made me feel alive again. Gaz taught me this move called 'the rock and roll', which was a 25-punch combination on the pads. After every session, I'd go home and all I could think about was this combination. I'd go to bed thinking: 'Tomorrow, I'm gonna nail it.' That's what kept me going back, day after day, week after week. It must have taken me two months to get this combination right. But when I did, the sense of achievement was invigorating.

I'd never boxed but I knew I could fight. When a fight goes off, whether it's in a nightclub or in the street, my heart rate goes through the roof. Gaz had four or five amateurs in his gym and after my session they'd climb in the ring and start sparring. I used to say to him:

'Come on, Gaz, are you gonna let me jump in or what?'

'Nah, you can't spar with them, these are good lads and you've got a game on Saturday. You'll get hurt.'

'They're not gonna hurt me, Gaz, they're only kids.'

This went on for a couple of months until I threatened not to come any more. So in the end he let me, and I absolutely loved it. Being in the ring didn't faze me but young kids of 14 and 15 were smashing me up in sparring. They'd turn up in their school uniform, change into their kit and dole me out some lessons, which was more embarrassing than anything. Gaz had a kid called JJ Bird, who was tipped for big things and used to batter me on a regular basis. He was really tall, had long arms and I couldn't get near him. But he went through what I went through in football, got involved with girls and drinking and took his eye off the ball. He turned pro but, lacking the love, his career petered out.

After a month or so of sparring, I started holding my own. After a few months, I was becoming a bit of a handful. I could always punch hard, but if you're not hitting anything, that's irrelevant. I had a classic boxer's frame – broad shoulders, long arms and slender legs. But my real strength was that I could absorb information and improve quicker than your average guy. So after a while, I was already thinking that boxing might be for me. The seed was planted.

'Gaz, how good are these kids?'

'These are good fighters, these lot.'

'But I'm doing all right against them, aren't I?'

'Yeah, you're doing all right . . .'

Gaz knew exactly what I was thinking, which is why he tried to play it down. He thought I had this perfect life as a professional footballer, that because I had loads of money, a nice car, a big house and a bit of fame, I must have been happy. But eventually I bit the bullet and came out with it: 'Gaz, I quite fancy having a go at this.'

'What, like a charity fight?'

'No, going professional.'

'Shut up, you idiot. What do you want to do that for?'

'But I'm doing all right against these kids, and they've been at it for a lot longer than me.'

'Curtis, they're taking it easy on you.'

'Don't say that, Gaz. Not if you don't mean it.'

'OK, you're doing well. But boxing is a hard, brutal sport and it takes a lot of dedication, determination and discipline. You're not ready, you're too old; you're going to be in with kids with loads more experience. And you're a footballer. Footballers don't box. My advice to you, as a friend, is do not do this . . .'

Nobody told me what to do. That skinny little kid on Northfield Crescent wanting to prove everyone wrong – 'FUCK EVERYONE!' – was back again . . .

'Barnes picks the ball up in his own half . . .'

'No way he's scoring this time!'

'Barnes goes past one . . .'

'Someone do the little bastard!'

'Barnes goes past a second . . .'

'Dare you to score!'

'Barnes has men free in the box . . .'

'Don't you dare make me look stupid!'

'Barnes goes on his own ... BARNES WITH ANOTHER ONE!'

... but, even I had to admit, Gaz had a valid point. It took a lot of dedication, determination and discipline to become a footballer, but no footballer had made a successful conversion to boxing before. In fact, the only sportsman I could think of who had made a successful switch to boxing was Anthony Mundine, the Australian rugby league international who had won a couple of genuine world titles. And his dad was a fighter. Plus, rugby league players tend to be a bit harder than footballers. Gaz must have thought I was nuts. But I sat down with him and explained that my life as a footballer wasn't what he thought it was and that I'd fallen out of love with the game a long time ago. And what else was I going to do? Buy a pub or a nightclub? It had crossed my mind but wasn't a very good idea, all things considered.

The day after I told him I wanted to turn pro, Gaz took me into his living room. It was the first afternoon of weeks of mental sparring.

'I've got some boxing videos; we'll watch a few fights if you like.'

'Yeah, sound.'

So we settled in on his sofa and watched a tape of the 50 worst knockouts you could ever imagine. Fighters out cold before they hit the deck, fighters knocked into the ringside seats, fighters sagging on the bottom rope, fighters staggering around the ring like drunks, fighters spraying blood from every hole. And after every knockout, Gaz looked over and raised an eyebrow, as if to say: 'That could be you.' I understood what he was doing and I appreciated his concern. But a few minutes after the tape finished, I turned to him and said:

'Gaz, you won the British title, didn't you?'

A big smile appeared on his face. That smile was enough for me. He wouldn't have swapped his boxing career, including the beatings, for anything.

Peterborough were relegated in 2005 and I played a massive part in that. The club was like an asylum, and if you stay in an asylum for too long you become a crazy person. Before I knew it, I'd taken the asylum over. I felt like Jack Nicholson in *One Flew Over the Cuckoo's Nest*. Between 3.00 and 4.45 on a Saturday afternoon was never a problem for me, but the rest was a disaster.

Bobby Gould was gone but what Baz knows about football tactics you could write on the back of a postage stamp. The ball was still being booted over my head and it wasn't as if we were winning – we were getting beaten pretty much every week. I'd say to Baz: 'Look, let's at least try to do it my way. Just give me the ball!' But nothing would change. Maybe the maddest part of the whole situation was that Baz knew his tactics weren't working either.

We won the first game that season and drew the second a few days later, after he told us to keep attacking when we were defending a lead and they scored a late equaliser. Nevertheless, it was a decent start, four points from six. But after that second game at Bradford, Baz sat us all down and said:

'Right, put your hand up if you think I'm an honest bloke.'

Everyone put their hand up, some more reluctantly than others.

'Right, I'm gonna be honest with you all now: this season, we will get relegated. We're fuckin' shit.'

When someone pointed out that maybe he'd got his tactics wrong, he went berserk: 'I'd rather lose 5-4 than win 1-0!'

I was sat there thinking: 'Fuck me, Baz, we're third in the league after two games and you've already given up! This is doomed . . .'

Sometimes, even after we'd won, he'd sit us all down and slag us off. He'd stand in the middle of the dressing room, with just a towel round his waist, point at one player at a time, starting with the goalkeeper, and say: 'You were shit . . . you were shit . . . shit . . . fuckin' shit . . . shit . . . fuckin' shit . . . fuckin' shit . . . shit . . . shit . . . shit . . . fuckin' shit.'

As soon as he was done, he'd walk out and you wouldn't see him for four days. Meanwhile, we'd all be laughing our bollocks off: 'What did you get? Shit or fucking shit?'

'I got shit. Happy days, I must have played a blinder . . .'

One thing I learnt from Barry Fry is that if you go nuts every week, people stop listening to you. Baz's ranting and raving just became boring. He'd call us all wankers after we'd won 3-0. 'Fuck off, Baz, you're an idiot.'

To be fair to Baz, he was manager, chairman and director, was part-funding the club himself and was probably on the point of having an aneurysm. He'd come in every week and say: 'Sit down, boys. Listen, I've got to tell you something: you're not getting paid next week, we've got no money. Not a fuckin' bean.' But we'd always get paid; it might just be a day or two late. Towards the end of my time at

Peterborough, Baz used to storm around the training ground wearing a pair of suit trousers, no shirt and nothing on his feet. This massive belly would be hanging over his trousers and he'd be ranting and raving on his mobile phone, calling some poor bastard every name under the sun. The players would be like: 'What the hell is Baz doing?' It was like a comedy sketch. The man was absolutely crackers. I reckon if you asked him about me now, he wouldn't even remember I was at the club.

As time went on, I became more and more disruptive. I was the captain and I was a terrible influence. I'd fallen out with coaches, was booting people in training, and all because I hadn't got my way. Sometimes, I wouldn't even turn up. The morning after my birthday, I was travelling down to training with Danny Sonner, who'd also been at Birmingham with me. We'd been on an all-dayer and drunk all sorts, so I was driving down the motorway, thinking: 'I'm not gonna make this, I must be 20 times over the limit.' So I got on the phone to Baz: 'Baz, it's Curtis.'

'Morning, Captain Marvel!'

'Baz, I don't feel like Captain Marvel today, mate. I'm rough as anything.'

'Oh yeah, weren't it your birthday yesterday?'

'Yeah.'

'Did you go out?'

'Baz, I got absolutely hammered.'

'OK. Stay at home, you can't train in that state. But we've got a game on Saturday, will you be all right for that?'

'Yeah, I think I will be.'

'All right, my son, see you then . . .'

This was Monday morning. He gave me the full week off. Because Baz knew I was his best player by miles, I had him over a barrel. Danny was sat next to me, rubbing his hands. We went straight back to the boozer ...

... Meanwhile, back in the real world, I'd take a stroll around Peterborough with Gaz after training, or we'd pop down to WHSmith to buy the *Boxing News*. And I noticed how people spoke to him – with respect. I'd hear them say: 'That's Gary De'Roux, he was a British champion.' And whenever there was an article written about me training with Gaz, it always started with: 'Gary De'Roux, former British champion ...' It made a big impression on me. Once you've become British champion, they can never take it away from you; it stays with you forever. I'd wanted to be: 'Curtis Woodhouse, former Liverpool captain and World Cup winner ...' That never happened. So I settled on: 'Curtis Woodhouse, former British champion ...' I liked the sound of that.

Gaz didn't start boxing until he was 21, so he must have known I had a glimmer of hope. But he still tried his best to put me off, pick the wings off the dream before it had a chance to take off. In a nice way, just in case it crashed and burned. He had me sparring this big heavyweight down in Kettering, who beat the shit out of me; he put me in with this tricky amateur southpaw who completely embarrassed me, even more than usual. But in the end I said:

'Listen, Gaz, I understand what you're doing. I know it's gonna be tough and might not work out. But I'm either gonna do this with you or I'm gonna do it without you. I'd love to do it with you, but if I have to go with someone else, I will.'

Gaz came round in the end. He knew I'd made up my mind. His most violent videos and any number of beatings wouldn't have stopped me. I think he just wanted to be there in my corner in case anything went wrong. He could see that I was happy. And unless you're happy doing what you do, life is shit.

CHAPTER 5

THE APPRENTICE

Sheffield, 1996

School wasn't my domain. I could sit in a class for hours and the teacher's words would go in one ear and out the other. I took three GCSEs and got an F in maths, an F in English and an A in PE, and 70 per cent of that was practical. But I always felt older and wiser than I was, ahead of the game, because of everything I'd been through. So I was always good at grasping the significance of certain moments. Driving with Dad from Driffield to Sheffield was one of them.

'Listen, son, this is it for you now. It's either this or you'll end up back with me. And you know what's happening where I am.'

An apprenticeship with Sheffield United wasn't just a chance to become a professional footballer – it was a chance to escape from Beirut.

'You don't want to go through all that shit. You have a great opportunity here and you are good enough to make it. I know I'm biased, but you're the best player they've got. Stop smoking and stop drinking. Don't fuck it up.'

I'd been boozing and smoking weed quite heavily from the age of 14. People assume boxing saved my life. Actually, Sheffield United saved my life. When I turned up there, I was already bang in trouble, because my life for the previous four years had been carnage. They took on a crazy one. But, Sheffield United being such a caring environment, the lid just about stayed on. That's why I love Sheffield United so much. Without them, who knows what would have happened. I'd probably be dead or banged up in prison.

When Russell Slade was nice to you, it usually meant you were about to get the mother of all bollockings. Russell Slade scared me shitless. Still does.

'Hiya, Curt.'

'Curt' – that's what he always used to call me when I was in trouble.

'Everything all right?'

'Yeah, sound, gaffer.'

Sat at his desk, I can feel sweat dripping down the small of my back.

'What you been up to today?'

'Nowt, just doing me jobs.'

'Right. Have you cleaned the balls?'

'Yeah, the balls are spot-on.'

'Bibs?'

'Yeah, the bibs are in the laundry room with Mary and Sue.'

'Don't forget you've got to clean the minibus as well.'

'Done it, boss.'

'Oh, right. Not been chasing anybody in it?'

'No, boss.'

'So you haven't tried to run over four Irish lads with the minibus?'

'No, boss.'

'Fair enough. Get yourself off if you want.'

'That all right, gaffer?'

'Yeah, have the rest of the day off. Put your feet up.'

As I get up to leave, he goes ballistic.

'Did you try to run those fucking Irish lads over?!'

'Gaffer, swear down I didn't!'

'Look me in the eye and tell me you didn't?'

Our eyes must be about an inch apart by this point. And Russ is not the prettiest of sights from 100 yards away.

'Gaffer, I promise you I didn't.'

'So are you calling Derek Dooley a liar?'

Derek Dooley was the chief exec at the time and a club legend.

'What's that, gaffer?'

'Derek Dooley was up in his office, having a board meeting, and he's looked out the window and seen you trying to run the Irish lads over!'

Rumbled. Irish apprentices were all the rage at the time and we had four of them. They were great lads, typical Irish, loved the banter. But for whatever reason they were getting on my tits. So I leaned out of the minibus window and said:

'If you carry on taking the piss I'm going to run you over.'
They carried on taking the piss. I couldn't even drive at the
time – I was only 16 – but I jumped in the front, turned the
key, put my foot flat to the floor and aimed right at them. I
swerved – not to miss them but to make sure I hit them –
went through the advertising boards and ended up on the
pitch. I managed to get it off again but I'd left big skid marks
all over the turf. I told Russ I was trying to park it and put
it in the wrong gear. But it wasn't just Derek Dooley who'd
seen me – it was the whole of the Sheffield United board. I
missed the lads anyway, so I didn't know what all the fuss
was about. But they still wanted to sack me.

I could have been sacked 10 or more times while I was
an apprentice at Sheffield United. But when you're the best
player, you get more lives than you should. My two years as
an apprentice were the best time of my life, by some distance. I'd escaped the mayhem back in Driffield and was
having a ball. In my first year, I was on £38.50 a week, and
we got paid monthly. For a week I used to live like a rock
star, then I'd ring up Dad and ask him to lend me 20 quid.
When I first turned up at Sheffield United I didn't even have
any trainers. I had some tracksuit bottoms and a pair of black
leather dress shoes. So with my first pay packet I bought a
brand-new pair of Nike Airs. They were 80-odd quid, so I
was left with about 80 quid to get me through the rest of the
month. So I sold my bus pass for 20 quid and used to hand
snide taxi receipts into accounts, to keep myself solvent.
After a while I was on about 500 quid a week. I'd dump this
big pile of receipts on Carol's desk and she'd laugh at me and
say: 'We can't give you all that, Curtis.'

'What can you give me?'

'We can give you a hundred.'

They knew what I was doing, just trying to get by.

I also used to go out nicking wheel trims with Owen James, who later became my strength and conditioning coach in boxing. We got caught a few times but never got nicked for it. Owen had an Escort XR3i, but it wasn't a real XR3i; he just used to nick all the gear for it down Abbeydale Road and soup it up so it looked like one. But it wasn't really about the money for me – I just found it exciting. I was still nicking wheel trims when I was in the first team. Problem was, because I was in the first team, people started recognising me: 'I'm sure I've just seen Curtis Woodhouse nicking some wheel trims . . .'

'Couldn't have been.'

I fancied myself as a bit of a wheeler-dealer, so I set up this little market stall back in Driffield. It was basically a jumble sale of jumpers and shirts I'd nicked from my mates. Eventually Russ pulled me into his office again.

'One of your team-mates' mums has been on the phone. Apparently you've sold her son's jumper. You've got to get that jumper back.'

'I don't know where it is, Russ, I haven't got a clue . . .'

Russ was the only person in football who scared me. But he also looked out for me, so I really respected him. If it sounds like I was off the rails as a kid at Sheffield United, God only knows where I would have ended up without Russ. When I did something wrong, he was the harshest on me out of all of them, probably because he felt I'd betrayed him. Russ was the best boss I had by a mile. He was getting on a bit when I first met him, so it's great that he's finally getting the recognition he deserves after great work at Scarborough, Grimsby, Yeovil, Cardiff and no doubt now at Charlton. If Russ rang me and said, 'I've got a game in a couple of hours and I need a midfielder, can you make it?', I'd be in the car like a shot and bombing down the motorway. Even in the state I'm in today.

I assumed all clubs were like Sheffield United and I thought football would always be as enjoyable as it was in those first two years. It was like a replacement family; I knew everyone and everyone knew me. When I was injured, I'd go drinking with Mary and Sue from the laundry on their lunch break. We'd go over to The Cricketers, opposite the ground, and sink four or five pints. They'd go back in and wash the kit and I'd sneak back in pissed.

All the apprentices used to stay in digs and eight or nine of us lived with a lady called Rita. Rita was brilliant – she looked after us like we were her own kids. But we used to call her 'Rita, the girlfriend eater' because she never let girls in the house. Luckily, she had this Turkish boyfriend called Ersan. He used to say to us: 'If you bring girls back, you tell me and I sneak her in.' So whenever we were going to bring a girl back, we'd ring Ersan and he'd open a window for us. We'd sneak them round the back and shove them in, which in some cases was like trying to shove a marshmallow into a money box.

I was a cocky so-and-so, had some serious front. After one youth-team game I walked up to Nigel Spackman, who was the first-team manager, and said: 'Gaffer, can I have a word with you? Why aren't I playing?'

We had a ball-winning midfielder at the time called Mark Patterson, who'd played something like 500 Football League games. I said to Spackman: 'I'm better than him.'

Spackman started laughing, walked over to Russ and asked: 'Who the hell is that?'

'Oh, that's Curtis Woodhouse, captain of the youth team.'

Next game, Spackman was on the sidelines. It was against Sheffield Wednesday at home and when I saw him standing there, I thought: 'This is it – if I play well here I'm in the first team next week.' I was so hyped up, I got sent off for a bad tackle after seven minutes. Russ tore strips off me in the dressing room, nearly made me cry. I respected him so much I hated making a mug of him. Not that I didn't keep on doing it, I couldn't help myself. But I knew, and everyone else at the club knew, that I was going to be in the first team soon.

Because I was making a few waves, I started getting a bit big time. I was supposed to be Wayne Quinn's apprentice, which meant cleaning his boots, putting out his kit, basically being his bitch. After a while, I just stopped doing it and Quinny had to replace me. Every Christmas, the first-team players would give their apprentices a bit of a tickle, but Quinny didn't give me anything. He made a big play of giving my replacement 100 quid, as if to say: 'That could have been you.'

One time, I was asked to clean the changing room and thought: 'You know what, I fancy a Jacuzzi and a massage instead.' I'd not even kicked a ball for the reserves yet but I tracked down Rob Strickland and said to him: 'Fancy popping down Swallow Nest for a Jacuzzi and a massage? We've had a hard week, we deserve a bit of a chill-out.'

It was only Monday.

'Nah, Russ will go mad.'

'Forget Russ, he's never gonna know.'

So there we were, sat in this health-club Jacuzzi, when the woman from reception came down and said: 'Is one of you Curtis Woodhouse?'

'Yeah, me. Why?'

'Russell Slade's on the phone for you.'

I just wanted to drown myself.

'You go and answer it, Rob. I'm not getting out.'

'He hasn't asked for me; you're gonna have to go and speak to him.'

So I put on a fluffy dressing gown and a pair of slippers and went along to reception.

'Hello, gaffer?'

'Hiya, Curt. You down at Swallow Nest?'

'Yes, gaffer.'

'It's lovely down there, isn't it?'

'Yes, gaffer.'

'Are you in the Jacuzzi?

'Yes, gaffer.'

'It's lovely and warm in there, isn't it?'

'Yes, gaffer.'

'After the Jacuzzi, have half an hour in the sauna, it's beautiful in there.'

'OK, gaffer.'

'What are you gonna do after your sauna? Get straight off?'

'Yes, gaffer.'

'Don't go back to your digs, pop by my office. But only if you find the time.'

When I walked into his office, he grabbed me by the neck, lifted me up and pinned me against the wall.

'You think you've arrived?! You've played 20 minutes for the Under-16s and you're sat having a fucking Jacuzzi when you should be cleaning boots!'

And I was thinking: 'Well, that's what the first team do . . .'

About as high as life got as an apprentice were nights out in the Europa. Everyone used to have Wednesdays off, so pretty much the lot of us would jump on a bus and pile in there on Tuesday nights. Because I looked really young and had this dodgy fake ID, with a picture that looked nothing like me, it was always 50:50 whether I'd get in or not. So when I did get in, I was determined to have some fun. I've always enjoyed ducking and diving, so I liked the fact I didn't have any money. That was part of the buzz, seeing how good a night I could have with only eight quid in my pocket. The first team would invariably be in there and I'd always tap up Mitch Ward or Dane Whitehouse: 'Lads, I don't have any money, lend us a tenner!'

'Here's 20 quid, now piss off.'

Dougie Hodgson, this big Australian guy, loved a night out and would always get the beers in for the young lads, and Don Hutchison would often give us a few quid to spend. Don used to call me 'Wiggy', because I had a big Afro at the time, and 'Huggy Bear', because he once saw me out wearing these wide, black trousers teamed with white loafers. He'd come over and say, 'Hello Wiggy/Huggy, you out with the lads?', and peel off 200 quid. They had this 'wheel of fortune' behind the bar. They'd spin it and if you got lucky, it was a pound a drink. That's a hell of a lot of booze, even between 20 of us.

They were great times, like we were on one, long holiday. Twenty lads doing something we loved, trying to fulfil the dream we'd had since we were young kids. Everyone with their little quirks, lots of piss-taking, every night out producing all these daft stories. Richard Tracey used to go out with a programme to prove that he played for Sheffield United – Under-16s. It was embarrassing. You'd see him speaking to some girl at the bar and he'd pull this programme out of his pocket, skip straight to the back and point out this tiny Under-16s match report: 'Look, look – we won 2-1 and I scored both of them!'

But I wouldn't want you to get the wrong impression. Although I can see how you might. There was a simple reason why I developed quicker than everyone else, and that was because I worked harder than everyone else. Loads of my childhood friends fell by the wayside in their teens, really talented kids. And loads of my fellow apprentices got released in 1997 – only three of us were kept on. A lot of them had become interested in cider and girls. And cider, girls and football don't really go together too well.

'Listen, Curtis, disco tonight. You coming?'

'Nah, I can't. I've got training tomorrow.'

'But Sally with the big tits is gonna be there!'

'Not bothered.'

Football was still everything to me and I hated losing. It went back to playing on the estate with the bigger lads. If I won, none of them could say anything to me. But if I lost,

I'd have to listen to them all day, calling me those names. I got sent off loads of times as a youth-team player. If I lost my head, I'd just go and boot someone. But only because the desire to win had overwhelmed me. I had tunnel vision. For me, it was like the World Cup every day.

CHAPTER 6

DO NOT PRESS!

Hull, September 2005

A manager with a tearaway player is like a woman with a rogue: they always like to think they'll be the one who finally tames him. But I wasn't willing to be tamed. Peter Taylor knew what a good player I was. He knew it was still in there somewhere and thought he'd be the one who redis-covered it. But if Hull's manager had been Bill Shankly it wouldn't have made any difference.

Hull were back in the Championship after back-to-back promotions. They had a shiny new stadium and there was a real buzz around the city. Plus, it was virtually my home-town club. A lot of my friends had season tickets and they'd be roaring me on from up in the stands. So I thought: 'Right, let's have one last roll of the dice. If I can't get up for this, then I know it's definitely over.' What else was I going to do? Work in a supermarket? There was no plan B.

Kicking a ball about was all I'd done since the age of 12. If you had dug through all that bitterness you would have eventually reached the love. But you would have been digging for weeks. Everywhere I went, I gave 100 per cent on the pitch. But because I hated it at the same time, I always found a way to sabotage things. If someone says to me, 'Whatever you do, DO NOT PRESS that big, shiny red button over there', I'll be sat there all day thinking: 'I wonder what that button does?' It would just nag away at me. Give it long enough and I'll press it in the end.

I made a slow start at Hull but after a few games on the bench, I finally broke into the team. The KC Stadium was like a morgue, the worst atmosphere I've ever played in. It held 20,000 but Hull only had about 5,000 hardcore fans, who were spread around the ground. Despite this, I was performing well. But I was still getting into plenty of trouble off the pitch. One time, this big lump started mouthing off in a bar, so I offered him outside. He was about 6ft 4in and I'm about 5ft 6in, but I nailed him with a shot and knocked him clean out. I turned to his mate and said: 'Do you want some as well, you little bastard?' Suddenly, he started hitching up his trousers. The next thing I remember was waking up in the back of a black cab and my mate laughing so hard he literally couldn't talk.

'What happened?'

'You've just been knocked clean out, mate.'

'How?'

'You got Jean-Claude Van Dammed!'

The little bastard had clocked me with a flying kick, right in the face. My lip was shredded, I was covered in blood. Apparently me and the bloke I'd knocked out were lying next to each other and the Karate Kid was chasing my mate, who was also about 6ft 4in, around the car park. It must have looked like a Benny Hill sketch.

Another Friday night we played Millwall at home and, because I won man of the match, I decided to celebrate in a local club. It was a fun night; I was having a good laugh and some dickhead went and spoilt it again.

'What the fuck are you looking at?'

I was facing the bar at the time.

'What the fuck are you looking at?'

I turned around.

'Yeah, you.'

'I'm not looking at anyone, pal, I'm just having a drink.'

After I left the club, one thing led to another and we ended up having a bit of an altercation. He landed on my fist and broke his jaw in six places. He was out cold for 10 minutes and they had to call an ambulance. The following morning, I was warming up before training and suddenly I saw a police car pull into the car park. I knew straightaway it was for me. Two coppers got out, had a quick chat with Peter Taylor and then arrested me. I've already got a rap sheet longer than my arm and now I've been charged with wounding with intent.

I was told I could have done 10 years. I told them exactly what happened, that this geezer started on me in the nightclub, followed me outside, started throwing punches and when I chinned him he must have fallen funny. Truth be told, it was one of the best left hooks I ever threw. Luckily for me, it was all caught on CCTV and this girl I went to school with, one of those plastic 'community' coppers, also witnessed it. She sent the police a statement, backing my story, and eventually the charges were dropped.

Problem was, that only happened four months later, by which time Hull had said to me: 'You know what, Curtis, this isn't for us.'

So that was that. Peter Taylor had taken a gamble on me and I'd lasted seven months. I didn't even speak to him before I left. Adam Pearson, the chairman, called me into his office, paid up my contract and I was gone. Sounds brutal. But if Mum or Dad got sacked, there wouldn't be money for food. When I got sacked, I was given a cheque for 18 months' wages. So not that brutal.

It turned out I wasn't up for it, after all. This loveless relationship wasn't getting any sweeter. It turned out I wasn't bothered where I played, who I played for and what badge I wore on my chest. I didn't want to play at all. I was torturing myself, dying a long and painful death. But I hadn't been ready to let go, until now. Getting Dad's blessing to quit football for boxing was a huge weight lifted from my shoulders. I'd been so worried about telling him, but he just wanted me to be happy and enjoy my life. Even if he didn't believe in it, it wasn't for him to say; it was for me to go and find out. There's nothing worse than someone pissing on your dream. Especially if he's your superhero.

Dad's twin brother, Carson, died of a stroke in 2002. The first attack paralysed him down one side of his body and left him in a wheelchair; the second caused bleeding on the brain and killed him. Uncle Carson was the first person to die who I was close to. It sent me reeling. But selfishly, my overriding thought was: 'Shit, what about Dad? They've got the same DNA, the same body frame, eat the same shit, drink the same shit. He should probably start looking after himself a bit better.' But he didn't listen to anybody.

While these charges were still hanging over me, and not

long after Dad gave me the nod to become a professional boxer, we were due to see Mike Tyson in a dinner show in Doncaster. Dad used to be late for everything and it would wind me up. So I gave him a call to chivvy him along: 'We're meeting Mike Tyson, remember – don't be late.'

'Don't worry, I'll be ready.'

I rang him back about half an hour before I set off.

'You ready? I'm on my way.'

'Yep, yep, I'm ready ...'

He sounded drunk. Or like he was in the bath. When I put the phone down I knew something wasn't right and immediately rang back. Nobody answered. I gave it two minutes and rang again. His girlfriend Julie picked up: 'Your dad's collapsed in the pub – there's an ambulance on the way.'

I went straight to Hull Royal Infirmary and discovered he'd had a TIA, or mini stroke. The doctor told me there hadn't been a bleed on the brain and he was going to be fine. It was essentially a warning stroke, nature's way of telling him to clean up his act. He had all these tablets to take; he was told him to stop smoking and eating junk. He didn't drink that much, maybe five pints a week. He just needed to start being a bit more careful. But a doctor telling Dad to clean up his act was a waste of oxygen. Dad was an alpha male, a silverback, and he didn't get told what to do, especially by a scrawny little doctor.

While he was still in hospital, I caught him smoking out the back. I was fuming.

'You've just nearly died and you're out here having a crafty fag. Do you ever think about anyone else? You're so fucking selfish.'

I could have been talking about myself.

CHAPTER 7

IN THE GANG

Sheffield, November 1997

When I was still an apprentice, I'd watch the first team play at Bramall Lane. They were a really good side at the time. They lost in the final of the First Division play-offs in 1997 and the following season the squad was full of former Premier League players, real proven, top-drawer performers like Brian Deane, Dean Saunders, Don Hutchison, Jan Age Fjortoft and Paul McGrath. But I'd sit in the stands and say to the other lads:

'They're a good side, but they'd be a lot better with me in it.'

'Shut up, will you? You're so big time.'

'I will play for the first team this season, I swear to God.'

I was so full of it, and so convincing, that they were probably thinking: 'He will do, as well.' So when Nigel Spackman rang to tell me I was being called up to the first team for the home game against Crewe, my first thought was: 'Fuckin' 'ell, what's taken you so long?' I was only 17. Even though it wasn't a shock, I was absolutely buzzing. The first thing I did was ring Dad: 'Dad, I've been picked for the first team.'

'Well done, son. About time.'

There was a bit of hype around me even before I made my first-team debut because it had been a fair few years since anyone had come through from the youth team. The last batch to make the step up were people like Dane Whitehouse and Mitch Ward, who were now 26 or 27. So when Spackman turned round to me and said, 'Curtis, go get warmed up', the fans went nuts. They were as excited as I was. I ran up and down the line for 10 minutes, sat back down next to Bobby Ford, and Spackman said: 'Get your gear off, you're coming on.' Not so cocky now. I shit myself. My legs turned to spaghetti and I remember actually thinking: 'I think I must be injured.' I soon got over it. And when I stepped on to that pitch for the very first time, it was like waking up from the most fantastic dream and realising it was all actually happening.

'Wow, I've done it ... I'm actually a footballer ... I've actually become a professional footballer ... I'm actually here now ... this is just too much ...'

I was only on for the last 20 minutes but we won 1-0. I acquitted myself well and, when Spackman put me on the bench for the next game against Stoke, I really felt part of the gang. It's all right training with the top dogs and tagging along with them on a night out, but it's only when you're actually in the team that you really feel accepted. I might have only been 17, but I knew I was good so was chirpy as anything. So chirpy, I think it frightened some of the old-timers. Inside I was a little bit apprehensive but I certainly wasn't intimidated. 'Just give me the ball and everything will be fine.' I'd be in the dressing room telling them all that I was better than them. Because they liked me, and because I was good, they just laughed. If you've got bravado and no talent, you'll soon get found out. Established pros are like bloodhounds – they'll sniff out the slightest weakness.

There were some star names in that team and some big personalities, but the Sheffield lads ran the dressing room: Dane Whitehouse, Mitch Ward and, before he left, Carl Bradshaw. They were Sheffield United fans; it was their football club, so they were in charge. People think managers run the dressing room but they don't, players do. We used to have two dressing rooms at the training ground, one for the young, in-crowd and another for the foreign and older players. The first one was full of absolute wrong 'uns: me and Quinny, Paul Devlin, Lee Morris, Bobby Ford – it was absolute carnage. Whenever it was someone's birthday, they'd get thrown in the boot room and bombarded with boots, buckets of water, anything anyone could get their hands on. Some of the pranks you could play on apprentices back then, you'd get three years for it nowadays. We had one apprentice called Paul Burke and, because he'd played for England Under-16s, we all thought: 'You big-time bastard.' He wasn't even that big time, he was a nice kid. But one day we stripped him down to his pants, smeared him with dubbin, banged him in the boot of a car and dropped him off in Sheffield city centre, outside McDonald's. He had to run all the way back to the training ground. Meanwhile, I'd have

Fiery Jack smeared in my pants, the legs cut off my trousers. I'd also get ribbed mercilessly about my clobber. I once bowled in with these black-and-white shoes that looked about four sizes too big for me and the place erupted. But I didn't give a shit, and that was the best way to be.

There were no rules; it was no-holds-barred banter. Jokes about mums, grannies, religion, race – nothing was off limits. One of the lads, who will remain nameless, used to piss down the back of people's legs in the shower. He'd do it to new players, just to make sure they were settling in OK. Saying that, he did it to me almost every week. Someone else would usually turn off the lights and I'd hear this fella whispering in my ear: 'That's what we used to do to black lads round here, back in the day. I think we should bring it back.' You wouldn't get away with that kind of thing now. You probably couldn't get away with it back then, except in that dressing room. Team-mates would say to me: 'What are you, Curtis, white or black? I'm not sure what you are.' And I'd sneak out and spray 'KKK' on their car. A few of the lads didn't appreciate that sort of stuff. When Marcus Bent joined the club a bit later, he'd walk in and the room would go silent: 'Did I just hear someone making monkey noises?' But I found it funny. I loved dishing it out and I loved taking it back. I was in my absolute element.

After I'd played a couple of games for the first team and just before we beat Charlton 4-1, I negotiated my first pro deal. I didn't have an agent at the time so it was just me in a room with the chairman and the chief executive.

'How does £250 a week sound?'

I thought: 'Pass me the fucking pen, where do I sign?!'

I was on £42.50 at the time so I thought I was suddenly made. I was bouncing off the walls. It never occurred to me that I'd been stitched up, because I didn't have a clue about money. I came from a council estate and never had a penny. I'd have to stand in the free-dinner line at school; I was the kid who had nothing. Nobody in my family had ever had any money and I'd never known anybody with any money. So they could have offered me 50 quid a week and I would have signed. When I was coming up through the ranks at Sheffield United, never once did money cross my mind. I wasn't thinking: 'God, if I make it, I'll be able to buy a mansion with 50 rooms and a couple of Ferraris.' I just wanted to be John Barnes. Even when I broke into the first team, I wasn't interested in what anyone else was on. I was just buzzing to be in the first team.

But a couple of weeks later, Lee Sandford, one of the club's old pros, took me aside after training.

'I hear you've just signed your first deal.'

'Yeah.'

'Happy with it?'

'Yeah, I'm buzzin'.'

'Can I ask you a personal question?'

'Of course you can.'

'How much have they given you?'

'£250 a week!'

I was proud as punch.

'You are joking?'

I thought he meant in a good way.

'And you've signed a five-year deal?'

'Yep.'

'So in five years' time, when you're averaging 30 to 40 games a season and you've played over 200 games for the club, you'll be 22 and still on £250 a week?'

'Shit . . .'

'Want some advice? Get yourself an agent.'

Not long after that, Lee Morris signed his first deal and his dad Colin found out what had happened to me. He got us both signed up with the agent Mel Stein, who used to look after – if you can call it that – Paul Gascoigne. Mel went straight to Sheffield United and threatened to sue them, so they ripped the contract up and gave me an improved deal of £2,000 a week with £1,000 appearance money. We were both 17, still living in digs and suddenly on three grand a week. Oh, plus a 100-grand signing-on fee spread over three years, which meant we had another 30-odd grand sitting in our accounts. It was like we'd won the lottery. Looking back, £250 a week made a lot more sense.

My real breakthrough game was against Stoke. We were 2-0 down at half-time; Nigel Spackman went mad in the dressing room, pointed at me and said: 'Get ready, you're coming on.' I replaced Mark Patterson, the guy I'd told Spackman I was better than in the first place, and he went ballistic. Mark was a bit of a hard nut and he started chucking all his gear about, shouting: 'You're bringing me off for this fucking gimp?!' I was sat there in the corner, shitting myself. I felt like saying: 'It's not my fault.' Before the start of the second half, Brian Deane stopped me in the tunnel and said: 'When you get the ball, put it in the box and I'll do the rest.' We pulled it back to 2-2 before I whipped in a cross from the left and Deano scored the winner. The place went absolutely mental. I made my first start in the next game – against Norwich away – got terrorised by a guy called Adrian Forbes and we lost 2-1. I played left wing-back but Forbes was strong and quick and made me look a bit silly. But it wasn't my fault; the gaffer should have played me in my proper position in midfield. That's probably what I thought. I was full of myself.

Norwich away was the first time I properly went out on the beers with the first team. We stayed over after the game, ended up in this god-awful nightclub and some of the lads set me up with this girl who was as big as a house. All the lads were taking the piss out of me but I ended up taking her back to the hotel and sleeping with her. That was my initiation ceremony, their way of introducing me to the team. It was better than being pissed on in the shower or stripped and dumped in Sheffield city centre. I loved every minute of it. I was sat there thinking: 'Jesus Christ, I'm out drinking with Brian Deane here!' Never mind the big lass; I was proud to be seen with them. I'd finally arrived.

CHAPTER 8

OF COURSE YOU ARE

Grimsby, January 2006

'**F**ancy coming to Grimsby?'

'What for, fish and chips?'

'Stop being a silly bastard. We're top of the league!'

'I can only do one season – I'm jacking it in to become a boxer.'

'Of course you are . . .'

When Russell Slade said Grimsby were top of the league, he was referring to League Two. If, for whatever reason, Jose Mourinho had been at Grimsby, I wouldn't have gone. But Russ was my first coach as an apprentice at Sheffield United and if it wasn't for him, I might never have been a professional footballer. I wanted to finish with the person I started with and pay Russ back.

Russ knew all about my latest brush with the law but he'd heard far worse. I never really felt like most of my managers gave a shit about me, which is why they got nothing back. But I liked Russ; he'd given me so much over the years. And if I liked someone, I didn't want to let them down. Russ did scare me, but I didn't want to do well for him out of fear. I wanted to do well for him out of respect. Like Dad, I'd hate for Russ to think I ever let him down.

A few months after signing for Grimsby, I went public with my intention to become a professional boxer. I'd already told a few people in football. David Holdsworth laughed in my face. He wasn't the only one. Leon McKenzie, who knew more than most about what a hard business it was, just seemed shocked. At Peterborough, after I'd turned up to training with black eyes a few times, Leon said to me: 'What's happening, Curtis, the missus been beating you up?'

'I've started boxing.'

'Fuck off!'

'Seriously. And I'm absolutely loving it.'

A few months went by.

'Still boxing?'

'Yes pal. I'm thinking about jacking in the football and giving it a go.'

He knew I liked a drink and wasn't the most dedicated athlete.

'OK ... Curtis, I know you can have a little row, but can you box?'

He didn't know how to take it. *Really?* You sure you want to do that?

The general consensus among the football community was that I'd finally gone and lost it. 'What the hell are you doing?! Is everything all right?' I can't think of anyone who said: 'That's a good idea. Good on ya.' Even I thought it was a bit nuts, because it had never been done and I had nobody to follow. But by this stage in my career, I didn't really have any friends in football so didn't really care what any of them thought. I'd come in for training, have a laugh with everyone, leave and do my own thing, which was mainly boxing. But I wasn't becoming a boxer for anyone else. I was happy that Dad was happy, but I was doing it for myself, my own wellbeing, self-preservation. I certainly wasn't doing it for fame or fortune. There's not much of that about in boxing.

I knew Mum wasn't particularly pleased. Having a boxer as a son is every mother's nightmare. But she didn't try to talk me out of it. She'd learnt a long time ago that I wouldn't have listened. She knew how determined I was, because I got a lot of my tenacity from her. I remember racing her at swimming when I was a kid, and she'd start sulking if I beat her. Years later, she told me she'd felt like dragging me under, just so she could win. So because she knew how my mind worked, instead of going on about how much she hated the idea, she lined up behind me, like a good mum should.

I knew the decision to quit football for boxing was going to hit me in the pocket; I just didn't realise how financially crippling it would be. But I also knew that if I could win the British title, the reward would be so much bigger than any amount of money. I'd spent most of my life with no money and the more money I earned as a footballer, the worse my life got. If my girlfriend Charlotte thought differently, she never let on. Charlotte never dreamed about me winning the British title. But you have to be selfish to be a successful sportsman. It has to be all about you, otherwise it's not going to work. That's why Charlotte was perfect for me.

She was six months pregnant with Isla when I told her I was going to retire from football and become a boxer. She barely batted an eyelid, because she'd rather I was doing something that made me content than something that depressed me but provided a certain lifestyle. I could go home and say, 'I'm going to become a ringmaster in a circus', and she wouldn't be overly bothered. 'Sound,' she'd say, 'ringmaster now, is it? What do you want for your tea?' She's never got involved in my *vida loca*; she just sits back and crosses her fingers. I needed that unquestioning support. I had enough doubts in my head. I was being beaten up in the gym by kids who didn't have any hairs on their nuts. I didn't need any extra negativity. Otherwise I might have said: 'You know what, I'll just go back to football. Just for the quiet life.'

Some would call me a male chauvinist pig, a dinosaur. I'm old-fashioned, and I make no apologies for that. Stuff like finances didn't seem like any of Charlotte's business. If there were any money problems, they were my problems. Her responsibility was to take care of the house, get the kids ready for school, cook and clean. Just like Mum. I don't know if that's right or wrong, but that's how it is in our house and it works for us. It would not suit my personality to have someone getting overly involved in what I was doing. Just let me do what I've got to do.

What Charlotte didn't know was that I was nowhere near as sure as I appeared. When it all came out into the open, my first thought was: 'Shit, what have I done?' I felt like I'd let so many people down, especially Dad. But the person I'd let down most of all was myself. I'd been born with a talent for football, given this golden opportunity to ensure that when I retire at 35, say, I'll never have to work again and my family will be secure. Looking back, that feeling of guilt was the perfect foundation. Guilt and wanting to prove everyone wrong. Just like that skinny little kid on Northfield Crescent, before I made it in football.

I'd been universally accepted as a good player once I'd established myself in football. But now I had people laughing at me and that hurt my ego. The general perception was: 'What an idiot – who does he think he is?' Thank God there was no Twitter in those days; I'm not sure how I would have handled the abuse. It was like I'd come out as a transvestite or something. Loud and proud!

On the boxing circuit, I was a freak show. When Gaz took me out on the road sparring, word would get round and the gyms would be rammed. Everyone wanted to see just how shit I was and even the little gym rats would have their sparring gear on. They all wanted their pound of flesh, all wanted a story: 'I battered Curtis Woodhouse the other day – that stupid prick who quit football for boxing.' And I did get battered, every day. I'm already telling people I'm going to win the British title – me, Gaz and his missus have even put a bet on it – and I'm being beaten up by kids who've come straight from school. I still had a year left on my contract with Grimsby and, because I'd played well for them, plenty of other clubs were after me. So the temptation to reverse the decision was huge: 'I've done a few daft things in my time but this tops of all them.'

It's not as if anyone was saying: 'Yeah, he's all right.' I was a terrible boxer. But ego trumped temptation: 'I'm not gonna let these bastards beat me. Fuck everyone.'

Cardiff, May 2006

'Thank God that's over with.' That was the overriding emotion after my last game for Grimsby and my last game of professional football. The fact we'd just lost a playoff final at the Millennium Stadium didn't muddy the waters at all. I was looking forward to never playing football again and doing something else. Not that I hadn't given everything for the cause. I played really well for Grimsby. Even now fans talk highly of me, and I was only there five months. Not many fans got to see me play at anywhere near my best. Between Sheffield United and Grimsby, most fans were served up a shell of what I could have been. But I probably only played well for Grimsby because I knew it was almost over. It was like I'd finally accepted the marriage was dead. Give each other a hug, wish each other good luck and go your separate ways.

I really wanted to go out on a high and help get Grimsby promoted. All my family were there, including my eldest son Kyle. Aside from Russ, there were some good lads in that dressing room and we should have beaten Cheltenham. We'd only just failed to gain automatic promotion on the final day of the season and finished six points ahead of them. But Michael Reddy, who was brilliant up front for us that season, was taken off with concussion 25 minutes into the game; Rob Jones had a shocker at centre half and I didn't play well either. In fact, I should have been sent off in the second half. Grant McCann went round our goalkeeper, Steve Mildenhall, and as he was about to roll it into the open net I bundled him over. Straightaway I thought: 'Bollocks, I'm off here. What a perfect way to end it.' But when the referee pulled out his card, it was a yellow, not a red. I think he went easy on me because he knew it was my last game and felt sorry for me.

We went down to a late goal by Steve Guinan and afterwards the dressing room was horrible. It wasn't just that Grimsby had lost the game and missed out on promotion to League One; it was the realisation that the team would be broken up. Something like 10 of the 11 players who started that game were out of contract at the end of the season and, because Grimsby didn't go up, the club didn't have the finances to re-sign most of them and the team struggled the following season. That was also Russ's last game in charge of Grimsby and I was gutted for him. I felt like I owed him for everything he'd done for me. But if we had been promoted, who knows, I might have given it one last shot. So, from a purely selfish point of view, it probably turned out for the best.

When I got out of bed the next day, I just felt lighter. It was like a great big monkey had been lifted off my back. Neil Warnock had predicted I'd be out of the game at 25. I'd just turned 26. And I couldn't wait to get on with the rest of my life.

CHAPTER 9

AS GOOD AS IT GETS

Sheffield, 1997/98

That Sheffield United side was as rough and ready off the pitch as it was stylish on it. Nigel Spackman had us playing 3-5-2 before it became a sexy formation, and playing it really well. The club played some of the best football in its history during my first season. We had Simon Tracey and Alan Kelly as goalkeepers, both of them were class; a Greek fella called Vas Borbokis at right wing-back – he was unbelievable on the ball, good enough to play up front and maybe the most talented bloke I played with; Wayne Quinn at left wing-back; Paul McGrath, Carl Tiler and David Holdsworth in defence; Mitch Ward, Dane Whitehouse, Don Hutchison and Nicky Marker – who was player of the season that year – in midfield; Brian Deane, Dean Saunders and Jan Age Fjortoft up front. It was a hell of a side, with stacks of experience, which must have made Spackman's decision to call me up a little easier.

I didn't see Paul McGrath train the whole time he was at the club. On match day, he'd walk into the dressing room at 2.30, jump in a hot bath for 20 minutes, get out of the bath at 2.55, put his kit on and be the best player on the park. But you wouldn't see him for the rest of the week. I didn't realise he had a real bad drink problem; I was only 17, not a man of the world. I was sat next to him at a Christmas do and, when I passed him the wine, he put his hand up.

'I can't drink that, Curtis.'

'Why? Do you want a beer or something instead?'

'No. If I drink anything you won't see me for a month.'

He was really quiet but a lovely fella. He played his last professional game when he was at Sheffield United so I went to his testimonial in Dublin. I knew he'd been a great player for Man United and Aston Villa but didn't realise how famous he was until I went to Ireland. When he got off the plane, it was absolute chaos. It was like when The Beatles first rocked up in America. He got mobbed; I've never seen anything like it, before or since.

At the start of 1998 I did my knee for the first time. I used to play head tennis with the youth-team coaches, Russell Slade, Steve Myles and John Dungworth. John was the best at the club and he wasn't even a player – he was the head-tennis king. One Sunday, the day after I'd played for the first team, me and Rob Strickland arranged to have a game with Russ and Steve. I stretched for the ball and felt something go in my left knee. I wasn't even supposed to be there, so I was thinking: 'How the hell do I explain this to the gaffer?'

I didn't want to get Russ and Mylesy into trouble either, so instead of telling anyone I went into training on the Monday and a minute into the warm-up went down clutching my knee. Dennis Pettit, the physio, came running over and said: 'Bloody hell, that's swollen up quick.' It was already the size of a balloon.

The operation was arranged for Thursday morning and they told me not to eat or drink anything for 12 hours beforehand. Problem was, Wednesday night was Roxy's night. Roxy's was a dive, cheap and horrible. And that was just the women. So the night before the op, I fell out of Roxy's at four in the morning. I'd had about 20 bottles of Holsten Pils and I fancied a kebab. About an hour after I got back to my digs, someone picked me up to take me to the hospital. When it came to anaesthetising me, they couldn't knock me out because I was spewing up Holsten Pils and doner kebab. So the operation was delayed and the club went mad at me. I told them I was really upset about the injury and had had a drink to help me cope. Because I'd only just broken into the first team and didn't want to lose my place, I rushed myself back too quickly. From having the operation to playing my next game was less than four weeks and I was told that nobody had ever come back that fast. Inevitably, I soon broke down again and that was my season pretty much written off.

As for the club, a season that promised so much turned into a bit of a shambles. Our two leading goalscorers, Brian Deane and Jan Age Fjortoft, were sold in the January transfer window. We played Sunderland on the Tuesday, had Wednesday off, came in for training on Thursday and Deano and Fjortoft were gone. Just like that. Mitch Ward, Carl Tiler and Don Hutchison also left, so the team got ripped apart midway through the season. And shortly after coach Willie Donachie joined Man City, Spackman quit. The chairman, Mike McDonald, came out all guns blazing, accusing Spackman of betraying the club and not being up to the job. But if anyone had been betrayed, it was Spackman. What kind of club sells a load of their best players when they're in the running for promotion to the Premier League?

Spackman might have been inexperienced but he was a very good manager, with bright ideas, and great for a young player like me. Somehow we still managed to scrape into the playoffs, but lost to Sunderland in the semi-finals. It was such a shame, but typical Sheffield United. They always find a way to fuck things up.

Football was mine and Dad's thing. Mum must have watched me play about five times and my sister not at all. I don't think they really understood how good I was. So when I broke into the first team, it probably took them by surprise: 'Blimey, he's playing every week!' After the divorce, I didn't see Mum or my brother and sister for about 18 months. But things eventually settled down. Dad moved to Hull and met Julie, and falling in love with someone else brought him some peace. It also made things easier for me, because it meant I could sleep at night and didn't have to see him all torn up and permanently on the brink of causing mayhem.

But those four years of chaos in Driffield had left permanent scars. I was on edge all the time, panicking for no reason. I'd be that kid again, sat at the top of the stairs, clutching my knees and waiting to cry, heart coming through my chest. A coin spinning in my head. Not long after joining Sheffield United, I was diagnosed with anxiety. Because I couldn't sleep the doctor gave me sleeping tablets, but they just made me drowsy and people assumed I was pissed: 'Curtis, look at the state of you. You really need to sort yourself out . . .' Those early years are when you learn to be you, so I was effectively branded for life. But my relationship with Mum did begin to thaw. For a long time I resented her, and my brother and sister to a certain extent: 'You fucked off and played happy families and left me in the middle of all that carnage.' But I started to understand why Mum wanted to be out of the situation she was in. She went through an awful lot of shit as well, so it was good to see her smiling.

Mum was, and still is, the landlady of the Old Falcon in Driffield. The locals love her; she's the life and soul of the party, always messing about. She thinks she's still 21, a bit like me. She'd always have the football on the telly when I was playing and be the typical proud mum, bragging to anyone who'd listen: 'That's my son up there.'

'It never is, Sue?'

'Yeah, that's our Curt . . .'

Obviously there was a flipside, when people would come into the pub and say: 'I've just seen your Curt . . .'

'What's he done now?'

But that mainly came later. Back then, life was about as good as it gets.

CHAPTER 10

THE MEXICAN WINDOW CLEANER

Peterborough, summer 2006

I wanted to be a boxer and now I was one. My God, it was lonely. Even towards the end, there was one thing I still loved about football and that was the dressing-room camaraderie. My favourite part of the day was that half an hour between 10.00 and 10.30 in the morning. If there was anything going on in the dressing room, whatever club it was, I was always smack-bang in the middle of it. It was the two hours of football that were the problem. And the 12 hours afterwards. That half an hour of dicking about in the dressing room was never enough.

I still had a good time in the gym, a laugh and a joke, but it was very different to football. Boxers can die in the ring, so the gym was a far more serious place to be than the training ground. But what I loved about the sport was that it doesn't matter what colour, race, religion or even how big or how old you are. You all bleed the same, you all bruise the same, you all break the same. And when you have a hard spar with someone, there's an instant respect. You've shared something intimate that only you two will ever know about.

People often ask me how far I could have gone in boxing if I'd taken it up as a kid. They say: 'Surely you'd have become a world champion?' The truth is, I'd have got nowhere. I wouldn't even have got my career off the ground. You need discipline to make it in boxing and I had no discipline when I was a kid. I could still do what I was doing in football, play at a very good level and earn a lot of money. But pro boxers have even more spare time than pro footballers. And imagine me going out three or four nights a week in the middle of a training camp. I would have got hurt. I probably would have ended up as one of those blokes in Dad's pub: 'I was a good boxer when I was younger . . .'

By the same token, it wasn't boxing that suddenly instilled discipline in me. It was the previous 10 years of being a footballer. If you don't learn from 10 years of fucking up, then you're an idiot. I might not be academically bright, but I'm a clever kid. I was able to analyse what went wrong with my football career and take those findings into my boxing career. I didn't underachieve in football because I didn't have the ability, I just lacked discipline. So I thought boxing could be the exact opposite: I knew I didn't have much natural ability, but I thought I could balance the scales by working harder than everyone else.

Giving up the booze was easy because I wasn't in the

same place as I had been. The more I hated football, the more of a fat drunk I became. And the more of a fat drunk I became, the more I hated myself. When people tried to talk to me about football, I'd change the subject. 'Hello, Curtis, how did you get on today?' 'Don't know, not really bothered. Who won the 2.30 at Haydock?'

After my last professional outing, I didn't watch a game of football for three years. I felt that bitter towards it. But now that I was doing something I wanted to do, I didn't feel like drinking. This might sound odd, but I never really enjoyed drinking alcohol, which is why I was never alcohol dependent. I just enjoyed people and socialising. But now that I was fit and strong, getting my highs in the gym and out on the road, I didn't need drink anymore.

Two days after Grimsby's playoff final in Cardiff, I signed a two-year deal with Frank Warren and went straight into training for my first fight. Gaz trained me hard, three or four times a week, and I quickly started to drop in weight. I was 13 stone when I walked away from football, a fat bastard from all that boozing, but Gaz soon had me down to about 11 stone. At least that was one positive. Even at the end of my boxing career sparring was tough for me. Imagine how tough it was at the beginning, when I had no idea what I was doing. I always had a good whack, but when you've got the big gloves on and your opponent's wearing a headguard, the amount of damage you can inflict is minimal. Sparring is far easier for a boxer than a pressure fighter, because a boxer always wants to keep it long. So I was still getting busted up in sparring by talented 15-year-olds. But I liked being around young, ambitious kids; their enthusiasm was infectious. And I knew that if I kept at it, I'd soon start getting the better of them.

I'd got myself into great shape and now I had a venue and date for my debut: a dinner show at the Grosvenor House Hotel in London on 8 September, to be broadcast live on ITV4. So I'm thinking: 'Jesus Christ, it's my first ever fight and it's going out live on the telly. To be honest, I could do without the extra pressure.' I'd been punched in the mouth thousands of times and lost a hundred fights. But if you have a fight in a car park and someone beats you, it doesn't matter because no one sees it. You can say you tripped and fell into a door. But in the ring and on TV, there's no hiding. This time, hundreds of thousands of people will be watching and most of them will be licking their lips, wanting me to get battered. 'What on earth does this footballer think he's doing?!' The fear of being exposed weighed heavy on my shoulders.

I've got the venue and I've got the date, but until I knew who I was actually fighting it didn't feel real. With four weeks to go, I finally found out. My first manager was Dean Powell, who was a Frank Warren man but managed Gaz back in the day and was sound as a pound. So it was Dean who made the call: 'I've found someone for you.'

'Who?'

'A fella called Dean Marcantonio.'

My heart sank.

'Fuck off, Dean, I know what you're up to – you're trying to stitch me up. There's absolutely no way I'm fighting a Mexican on my debut.'

'He's not a Mexican, you dozy cunt, he's a window cleaner from London. Even better, he's fucking useless. He fought one of my other guys last week and made him look like Sugar Ray Leonard.'

'Is he a front-foot or a back-foot boxer?'

'He's no fucking foot! He's pretty much the worst boxer in Britain.'

Now it felt real. I didn't care that Dean Marcantonio was a window cleaner from London; I didn't care that he'd only had two pro fights. In my head I built him up to be this monster. I was nervous when I went to bed, thinking: 'Shit, I know nothing about this kid. And I'm fighting him in four weeks.'

There was a bit of a media storm during the build-up to the fight, a lot of stuff written about this footballer, a former England Under-21 international, jacking it all in to become a boxer. So that ramped up the pressure. But I felt fine the day before. I was a little bit nervous at the weigh-in, but that was to be expected; I'd never done this before. I was in great shape, scaled in at 10st 10lb, and the window cleaner wasn't as big as I'd imagined he would be and looked a bit podgy. I remember thinking during the face-off: 'I can take this geezer.'

After the weigh-in, me, Dad, my brother and Charlotte checked into the Grosvenor. Posh place, the Grosvenor, on Park Lane. So the person on reception must have been thinking: 'What's going on here, then – three black blokes and a glamorous blonde bird.' Charlotte said she felt like a high-class hooker.

London, September 2006

The laughter stopped when I arrived in the ballroom on fight night. It was a black-tie show for charity, which Frank Warren puts on every year. And it was absolutely packed. I'm looking around and I see Chris Eubank, Jonathan Ross, a collection of legendary boxers and big celebrities. And slap-bang in the middle of all these tables was the smallest ring I'd ever seen. I'd never seen a proper, professional boxing ring in real life and they looked massive on the TV. So now I'm getting nervous and a little bit paranoid, thinking that people are trying to stitch me up, that it's one big hoax for the benefit of ITV's viewers.

During my warm-up in the dressing room, I was managing to keep a lid on it. Gaz was trying to keep me calm while he was bandaging my hands and suddenly there was a knock on the door. It was Ernie Draper, the chief whip.

'Curtis, you're on in two minutes.'

I went as white as a sheet. I could almost feel the blood draining downwards out of my face. And I suddenly felt really tired. All that nervous energy just evaporated. It was horrible, the worst feeling of my life.

'You're not ready, Curtis. You're just not ready. What if it goes wrong? In front of all these people. What a twat I'm going to look. Everyone is laughing at me as it is. I don't want to be the laughing stock of the nation. "Remember that prick who packed up football to become a boxer and got knocked out in his only fight?" Maybe I can run away? How are you gonna explain that one? Imagine the headlines: "SHITHOUSE WOODHOUSE GETS THE RUNS!"'

Where had that kid from 24 hours earlier gone, the one who was full of confidence? I thought it was going to be great: 'I've watched *Rocky* hundreds of times, it's easy. Get in there, bash him up and then go and party.' I didn't factor in the nerves. I didn't factor in a lot of things. I'd done loads of sparring, loads of pad work, loads of running, loads of interviews. I'd pretty much mastered the interview. The fighting was almost an afterthought.

Walking to the ring, I was absolutely petrified. When I saw the ring steps, I thought: 'I'm not gonna be able to get up them, my legs feel hollow, like they've got nothing in them.' I've never been on death row and I hope I never will be. But I felt like a condemned man being led to the electric chair. During the face-off, my knees felt like they were knocking. You could probably hear them on TV, that and the sound of cutlery on crockery. When the bell finally sounded, I just wanted him to hit me as quickly as he possibly could. The anticipation is a lot worse than it actually happening. I just wanted it over with: 'Just hit me and let's get out of here.'

I don't remember much about the fight. But I do remember closing my eyes, winging away, hoping for the best and being level after two rounds. This is supposed to be the worst boxer in Britain and we're involved in a life-or-death struggle and inseparable heading down the stretch. But in the fourth and final round, I put him down with a left hook and it felt so, so good, almost like an ejaculation. And finally it felt like I'd put some distance between us. When

I put him down again with the same shot it felt even better. Surely I'd done enough.

Still, when the referee raised my arm the overriding emotion was relief. Back in the dressing room, I was absolutely shattered. We'd only fought four two-minute rounds and I felt like I'd just done the Thrilla in Manila. I left absolutely everything in that ring. So there I was, flat on my back in the starfish position, and Dean Marcantonio walked in, fresh as a daisy, not a mark on him.

'Fuckin' 'ell, you all right, son?'

'Fine thanks.'

'If you're ever down in London and need any sparring, give me a shout.'

He shook my hand and skipped off. And I was left thinking: 'I've just fought the worst boxer in Britain and he's come out of it better than me. Where does that leave me in the pecking order? Someone get me out of here . . .'

At least now I was a professional fighter. Afterwards, all the journalists were asking if I was going to fight again. They still thought it was a phase I was going through, that now I'd scratched the itch I'd go back to football. But even though I knew I was a million miles away from my goal of becoming British champion, the ambition remained the same. When I was a kid, I was a million miles away from playing professional football, but I made it. And I still thought I had something great, deep inside of me. So I told them: 'I'm in it for the long haul. No going back. I'm ready to go again.' Fuck everyone.

That night was one of my favourite nights in boxing. I'd love to tell you a poignant story about what Dad whispered in my ear straight after the fight, but us Yorkshiremen aren't big on slushy stuff and all that hugging people do down south. He probably said to me: 'Well done, son, what do you want to drink?' The fact that he was there and had paid 200 quid for a hotel room was enough. We had some good food and a few beers and I just let it all sink in. The following day we had an all-dayer in Dad's pub and he put the fight on loop on the big screen. That was Dad's way of saying how proud he was. It wasn't easy to watch, because frankly I was shit. But even though that fight was possibly the worst 45 minutes of my life while it was all happening, with hindsight it became brilliant. It's like going on the big dipper: when you're in the queue, you're shitting yourself. Once it's done, you want to jump straight back on again.

CHAPTER 11

THE CIRCLE AND
THE CROSS

Sheffield, 1998

I'll never forget the day it all changed. You might call it the beginning of the end. It was a Tuesday afternoon and Wayne Quinn said to me:

'You coming out tonight?'

'No, no, no, I'm all right. I've got training tomorrow.'

'Don't be a pussy, don't matter, we'll go out.'

He twisted my arm and about four or five of us went to a club called The Leadmill. It was the first time I'd been out with the first-team lads on a school night. And it was absolutely brilliant.

I'd played about 20 games for the first team and was pulling up trees. And because I'd come through the Sheffield United system, the fans loved me even more. I had a special bond with them. So when I walked into this club, I got mobbed. It was unbelievable. I felt like John Travolta in *Saturday Night Fever*. On my best day, looks-wise, I'm a solid five out of 10. And that's after a proper wash and shave. But when you're playing for Sheffield United, you're only 18 and everyone knows you're minted, you suddenly become a 10. Quinny was a handsome lad, looked like he was in a boy band, so some women probably had him down as an 11. And just in case any girls in there didn't know who I was or what I did, I was wearing this gold chain with a Sheffield United blade emblem dangling off it. If you had one of those round your neck, you were nailed on. There were women all over me. But at that point I was still naive. I thought little mixed-race kids with yellow teeth and shit clothes were suddenly in vogue.

I woke up the next day after partying all night and I should have thought: 'I need to sweat this out and get an early night.' Instead, I rang Quinny after training and said: 'Fuckin' 'ell, Quinny, last night was one of the best nights ever. Are we going out again tonight?' Quinny loved going out – he was one of the greatest goer-outers ever – so he didn't need persuading.

Before I knew it, I was going out three or four times a week. None of the senior pros took me aside and told me to behave and be careful because they were always out as well. It wasn't a dirty little secret, that's just the way football was in those days. We'd train Tuesday morning, go out en masse on Tuesday night and drink all day Wednesday. It wouldn't be three or four of us – it would be 15 or 16 of us. You weren't forced to go out; everyone was just like-minded. Even the players who didn't go out with the rest of the squad went out. You'd be in a club at two in the morning and spot Vas Borbokis sitting in the corner on his own, this little smile on his face. So it wasn't like anyone was saying: 'God, have you heard what he's been up to?' It was: 'God, have you heard what that 15 or 16 have been up to? Class!' And it's not like the gaffer didn't know about it – this was all going on in the middle of Sheffield. It simply wasn't frowned upon, nobody was breaking any rules. So I never once thought: 'I'd better rein this in a bit.'

And the reason we never fell behind other teams in the league was because they were all doing it as well. This was before the mass influx of foreign players and Arsene Wenger's more enlightened methods at Arsenal started to become the norm. We didn't have a nutritionist at Sheffield United. We didn't even have a canteen. We used to finish training, have steak and chips down the pub, a few pints, and then maybe hit the brothel. And you could hit the brothel safe in the knowledge that nobody would ever find out about it, because there were no mobile phones and there was no social media. I do have sympathy for players nowadays; everywhere they go, people are taking pictures of them and sticking them on Facebook and Twitter. They're young men, who fancy a night out every now and again and might only be having a couple of beers.

Footballers have an awful lot of time on their hands – most days they've finished work by 12.30. That's why old-time footballers almost all gambled, liked a drink and were handy at snooker. Because, let's face it, what else were we going to do? After training, I'd be in the bookies for the first race. Happy days. I take my hat off to the dedicated ones. After training, Brian Deane would do strength and conditioning at Don Valley Stadium. He used to ask me to go with him: 'Sorry, Deano, I've got the 1.35 at Kempton – can't miss that.'

A few would sit at home watching *The Simpsons* or playing computer games, tucking into a bowl of pasta. But that's not really me. If we're going to play a game, let's have a game of cards or snooker or dominoes and have a few pints while we're at it. And how can you be lounging at home watching TV or playing computer games when you know that if you step outside, you can be a rock star for a few hours? Jump in the shower, call Quinny, ring for a taxi – BEEP! BEEP! – 'Fuckin' 'ell, I'm going out again!' It's hard to look back on those early days with too much regret, because it was great fun. And, because I was only 18, it never affected me – I could still train at full tilt. I thought I was invincible.

It wasn't the money that changed me. I had more money in my pocket but I didn't go out and buy a posh car or a big house; I was still in digs a year after I made my debut. These days kids get all sorts of financial guidance but when I signed my first deal, there was no: 'Listen, you've got an awful lot of money now, you're probably best to invest it in this and avoid spending it on that.' They handed me a pen, I signed on the dotted line, was suddenly on 400 grand a year and wandered off into the jungle. I did have someone set up a few direct debits for me but I didn't even know what direct debits were. In our house in Driffield, we had to put 50p in the meter to get four hours of TV (we actually used Laura's toy plastic money, which gave them a shock when they emptied it once a month). So when all this money started leaving my account, I went to see one of the academy coaches, Paul Archer.

'Paul, I think somebody has hacked my bank account. Look at this bank statement: all this money is coming out at the end of each month, hundreds of pounds, and I'm not spending it.'

He looked at me like I was a Martian.

'Mate, they're your direct debits.'

'What do you mean?'

'Well, this one here is your phone bill ... this one here is your gas and electric ...'

When I moved into an apartment below Quinny in Tapton Mount (we liked to stay close to each other, in case we needed a night on the booze, and it was where the students used to go out – location, location, location ...) I now had a mortgage and had to pay council tax and this, that and the other. But I had no idea what a mortgage was. I didn't have a clue about anything.

I was still a teenager, so most of my money went on booze, birds and clothes, although my team-mates used to call me 'Scruff' because I could put on a five-grand suit and still look like a bag of shit. I've got that special talent. I'd also spend money on daft things. I'd go go-karting and spend hundreds of pounds because I'd want to keep going round all day. We went paintballing once and I won 'Rambo of the Day' because I bought that many hand grenades and smoke bombs. No wonder they gave me a medal – I must have doubled their takings for the month. I just used to enjoy enjoying myself, no matter what the cost.

But it's not the money that made the memories; it was the friendships and the team spirit. That flash culture you see in football today didn't really exist in my day, at least not in the First Division. Simon Tracey had this big, horrible old Mercedes. I used to take the piss: 'Has someone ordered a taxi? There's a big, horrible old Mercedes waiting outside.' Dane Whitehouse had a BMW M3 but that was the best motor in the car park by a long way. It was a very earthy dressing room, containing quite a few Yorkshiremen. If anyone had turned up in a Ferrari somebody probably would have keyed it.

But you didn't need a flash car or a big house to pull women – the knowledge that you were a footballer was enough. They just assumed the rest. And I'd never been backward in coming forward with girls. I lost my virginity when I was 12. It was after school, about four in the afternoon. I was probably still wearing my uniform, my tie swept over my shoulder. It wasn't my best performance but I got the job done and used to remind my mates about it every day.

If you're a footballer, you can look like Quasimodo and have your pick. When someone asked him what he'd be if he wasn't a footballer, Peter Crouch was bang-on when he replied: 'A virgin.' It's so easy for a footballer to pull women it almost takes the fun out of it. And if, for whatever reason, you were struggling, you'd just whip out your player pass, which they give you when you sign pro forms. Having your player pass on a night out was vital. When it got to two in the morning and you were desperate for a pull, that was when you went for your pass.

One night I pulled this girl who wasn't the best. So much so that loads of my team-mates had been denying they'd slept with her. When I got back to her house, I noticed there was a Sheffield United team poster above her bed. Over some players' heads there was a circle, over other players' heads there was a circle and a cross. So I said to her: 'What are all those circles and crosses on the poster?'

'Oh, you don't want to know.'

'Oh, I do.'

'OK then. The ones with a circle over their heads, I've given 'em a blow job. The ones with a circle and a cross, I've shagged 'em.'

Out of a squad of 35, about 30 of the lads had something over their heads. So I went and got a circle and a cross myself.

CHAPTER 12

OBSESSION

Bridlington, April 2006

After scraping past the Mexican Window Cleaner, I found a job cutting hedges by the River Humber with a Polish bloke who spoke no English. And they said going from football to boxing was drastic. I say I found a job, but really it found me. Just like trouble always seemed to do.

I'd gone to Bridlington for my brother's birthday. When I'd just got off the train and left the station, some coppers approached me. One of them said:

'You're under arrest. You've been caught on CCTV assaulting a member of the public in town.'

'It's not me, you've got the wrong person. I've just got off the train. I've only been here 30 seconds. I've not had one drop of alcohol.'

I showed him my train ticket and tried to walk past him.

'Sorry, we're going to have to take you in.'

One of the coppers tried to grab hold of me so I told him: 'Get your fucking hands off me, or I'll put my hands on you.' He tried to grab me again and the next thing I know it's all gone off. There were four of them piled on top of me, two on my legs and two on my back, and another one was holding my hands behind my back. While I was down there, a female copper knelt down and sprayed CS gas in my face – to 'calm me down'. That didn't work. It took them 25 minutes to get me in the van. When they announced that in court, I thought: 'You earned your money that night, you bastards.'

I ended up in the cells. But I had absolutely no remorse. What I did think was: 'Here we go again. I'm finally doing something I love and now I've been charged with assaulting six police officers. I could do time for this. It could all be over almost before it's started.'

During the hearing, the police admitted that what they arrested me for – assaulting a member of the public – I hadn't done. They also dropped the drunk and disorderly charge, because not even I can get drunk walking from a train station to a pub. But I did get done for assaulting a police officer, which, as far as I was concerned, they brought on themselves by wrongly arresting me. When people hear that a boxer has assaulted a police officer, they assume he's done some serious damage, which I hadn't. They tried to make me sound like the second coming of Roberto Duran. I felt like saying: 'Actually, I'm shit. There's only one boxer shitter than me in the whole of Britain, and that's Dean Marcantonio.'

But even though there were six of them in court, not one

had a mark on them. Either I'm a dangerous professional fighter or I'm not – they can't have it both ways. Even so, the copper I pushed apparently had to have two weeks off work. If I had my time again I would have chinned him. Might as well have done – the sentence would have been the same.

They gave me 200 hours' community service and the British Boxing Board of Control told me I couldn't resume my career until I'd knocked off my hours. At my initial meeting with the Board of Control, I'd told them I didn't have any court cases pending. So they thought I'd lied to them. In fact, the incident with the coppers happened literally a week *after* that meeting. But my pleas of innocence fell on deaf ears and I was a professional boxer no more.

Hessle Foreshore, January 2007

So here I was cutting hedges by the River Humber with a Polish bloke who spoke no English, when I wanted to be grafting in the gym. When it got to lunchtime that first Sunday, we still hadn't said a word to each other. I was sat there eating the lunch Charlotte had packed for me and I poured him a cup of tea to break the ice. He seemed to like it, but he didn't say anything. 'Jesus,' I thought, 'I hope I'm not paired with this geezer again next week.' As luck would have it, the next week I was paired with this geezer again. It got to about 9.30 in the morning and he suddenly said to me, with this big smile on his face: 'You want tea?'

'Yeah, I'll have a cup of tea, pal.'

I took a slug of it and it almost blew my socks off.

'Whoa, what the hell is this?!'

'This is vodka. In Poland, we drink vodka like you drink tea.'

So me and this Polish guy got absolutely bongoed together for the next 10 weeks. We couldn't really understand each other, but we communicated in the universal language of vodka. And it was strong shit. When I wasn't downing vodka with my Polish drinking partner, I was getting mortal drunk with some of the other guys in a pub at the bottom of the foreshore. We'd get back on the bus at the end of the day completely out of our heads. It was the best 200 hours of community service I'd ever done.

The real punishment wasn't the 200 hours of community service – the real punishment was having to go back to football. My heart was heavy but I needed the money. I had a family to support and a big house in Hull that needed paying for. It was either football or going back to nicking wheel trims. Nicking wheel trims would have given me a bigger buzz but I was better at football.

When I first signed for Peterborough, there was a businessman behind the scenes called Colin Hill. Colin sponsored me with my boxing, on the basis that if I ever came back to football I'd play for a team he was involved with. It just so happened that his brother, Garry, was manager of Conference side Rushden & Diamonds, so when Colin found out what had happened he gave me the call. I played well for Rushden that first season; it was easy. I was still good enough to be playing Championship football and I was in the best shape of my life. If I'd had my boxing fitness at the start of my football career, I'd have been a machine.

More importantly, I got more money at non-league Rushden than I did at Hull City. No wonder they ended up going under. My mind was nowhere near the actual football. When the whistle went at three o'clock I always gave my best, but it was only ever about the readies. At 4.45, I was out of there and on the motorway by five. I'd become a footballing mercenary.

Meanwhile, I'd had to leave Gaz after just the one fight. When I was training with him, I'd rented a house in Peterborough, living there Monday to Friday and going home at weekends. That was bad enough, because Isla had just been born and Charlotte was looking after two kids. After I lost my licence I had no reason to stay in Peterborough, so I returned to Hull. But travelling back and forth between Hull, Peterborough for boxing training and Northamptonshire for the football was just too much and it was costing me a fortune. It wasn't easy telling Gaz I needed to train elsewhere; him and his missus had been very good to me. But he wanted what was best for me. So I spoke to Dean Powell and he said: 'How far are you from Rotherham?'

'About 40 minutes.'

'Perfect. There's a trainer there called Dave Coldwell who you might be able to work with. I'll have a chat with him and see what he can do.'

I didn't really know too much about Dave. Before I made my debut, I met him at a fight in Barnsley. Ryan Rhodes was fighting that night and Dave was training him. They took me into the dressing room and Ryan was getting his hands wrapped. I was like: 'Jesus, it's Ryan Rhodes ... One of my boxing heroes!' First thing he said to me was:

'You must be fucking crazy giving up football for boxing.' While I was fighting Dean Marcantonio, Dave and Ryan were texting each other: 'That footballer's on TV, the one we met in Barnsley – he's absolutely shit!' Apparently, when Dean Powell spoke to Dave about me, Dave's first reaction was: 'What do I want to train a prima donna footballer for? I haven't got time for that.' Three weeks later, I turned up at his gym.

The first day I walked in, Dave said to me: 'Curtis Wood-house? The footballer?'

'That's me.'

The next day, he turned to me and said: 'You're sparring today, mate. Jump in.'

This other kid was already in the ring, with all his gear on. He was smaller than me, so I thought I could handle him. But in three rounds, he did things to me you couldn't even do on the pads. He was hitting me with every shot in the book, putting together daft combinations I'd only ever seen in computer games. Five-shot combinations, head and body, winding up punches, Ali shuffles, the works. It was like boxing Sugar Ray Leonard. I was wobbling all over the ring, gloves covering my face, scared – and too knackered – to throw a shot. I was nothing but a punchbag that day; he took me apart. And all the time I'm thinking: 'Jesus Christ, how good is this kid?'

Afterwards, sat on the apron, I was panting like a dog and sweating like a pig. I'd been taken apart but was pleased with the workout. No disgrace – I'd only had one pro fight and I knew Dave was looking after some good young kids.

'Fuckin' 'ell, he's good, Dave.'

'Yeah, he's good is Thorpey. Although he hasn't won a fight for a year.'

'How many fights has he had?'

'Overall? About 80. And he's only won about 10 of those.'

My heart sank. If I'm being taken apart by a journeyman, a kid who gets paid for losing, where does that put me in the pecking order? When I was a kid, I always said I was going to play football for Liverpool and England. And I truly believed I would. The dream never looked like this. What am I doing here? Where am I going with this?

I'd told myself I was going to be British champion. Suddenly, I realised how far away from completing the journey I was. 'What if this goes wrong? Then what am I going to do?' But my arrogance told me I still had something great in me. I just needed to prove it. I'd committed to the journey. People had laughed at me. And that was brilliant. I was back to being that 10-year-old kid playing football on Northfield Crescent: 'I won't let the bastards beat me.'

The next day, Thorpey texted Dave: 'Get me Curtis Woodhouse for my next fight – it's a guaranteed win.' I'm a laughing stock. Fuck everyone.

Dave reckons that when I first walked into his gym, I was one of the five worst fighters he'd ever seen. And he'd seen thousands of them. A willingness to fight might be in the genes, but boxing isn't. There is just so much to learn. But the one thing that Dave could turn to his advantage was that I was almost a blank canvas. Sometimes trainers will get hold of amateurs with all sorts of bad habits they can never iron out. I didn't really have any bad habits because I didn't even pretend to know what I was doing. The first thing he did was switch me from southpaw to orthodox. I'd made my debut as a southpaw, because I'm left-handed, but I never really felt comfortable boxing that way round. Saying that, I didn't feel comfortable boxing orthodox either. But having my left foot out in front felt more natural. And that's why I ended up with a good jab and a good left hook.

But when I first started throwing right hands as my backhand, I couldn't do it. I slapped with it for 12 months, dropped it downwards like I was throwing a ball. Dave would stop me on the pads all the time and it pissed me off.

'Just let me do what I'm doing.'

'No, Curtis, you've got to get it right . . .'

When I turned pro with Gaz, I became the only pro in his gym; the rest were amateurs. At Dave's I was surrounded by top fighters – a former British champion in Ryan Rhodes, a future world champion in Kell Brook, an experienced journeyman in Daniel Thorpe, good up-and-coming kids like Nav Mansouri and Jerome Wilson. So it was intimidating. Not necessarily physically intimidating, but awkward and unsettling. I could have walked into pretty much any football club and been confident in my ability to hold my own. But in Dave's gym, I wasn't very good and I couldn't hide it. I was looking at the other boxers and thinking: 'Shit, they're good.' And they were looking at me, poking away at the bag, trying to learn something new, taking ages to get it right, and thinking: 'Christ, he's shit.' Nobody ever said anything, but that's definitely what they were thinking because that's what their eyes were telling them.

It was uncomfortable at times, but at least now I had a

reference point. At least now I knew what level I needed to get to if I was to become British champion. And at this stage everything was new and exciting. I hadn't been worn down by the game yet; I was intrigued, still trying to work things out: 'Wow, how did he do that?' I wanted to learn how to do what the other boxers could do. It became an obsession, and that's what it needed to be. Almost a religion. There was no magic wand that made me better; I was just willing to spend more time in the gym than everyone else. People used to come in for an hour and a half and leave. So I'd think: 'If they're doing an hour and a half, I need to be doing three hours.' Maybe an hour and a half of hard graft and an hour and a half of learning. When everyone else had left, I'd still be working on technical stuff: right hand, turn it over, right hand, turn it over, right hand, turn it over ... It could be boring, but sooner or later I'd find some snap and the boredom would be replaced by this tremendous sense of achievement: another step taken.

CHAPTER 13

WHO IS THIS
LITTLE BASTARD?

Sheffield, September 1998

If I could bottle the feeling of scoring my first goal for Sheffield United, I'd be a billionaire a hundred times over. It wasn't particularly pretty: the Crewe goalkeeper fumbled a cross, Bobby Ford headed the ball back into the area and I stuck it in from about three yards out. I'd been planning that moment since I was a kid on Northfield Crescent. It wasn't the Kop I'd dreamed of, but it would do. Yet when it happened, I had no idea what to do. It was like I'd been paralysed with ecstasy. 'Shit, what do I do now?' So I jumped into the crowd. I completely lost the plot, was roaring my head off. They must have been thinking: 'What the hell is this kid on?! He's gonna turn into the Incredible Hulk in a minute!' A kid from the Sheffield United academy scoring his first goal for the club and celebrating with fans at the Kop end. I can't even begin to describe the feeling.

That 1998/99 season was my best for the club by far. In fact, it would turn out to be my best season in professional football. And I was only 18. Steve Bruce had taken the manager's job the previous summer and I got on really well with him. The bloke was a Man United legend, so I hung on every word he said. It was his first management job and he could still play a bit. I thought Steve Bruce could only head and boot it but he was excellent technically. Saying that, I remember getting beaten 4-0 by a great Sunderland side at Bramall Lane and Michael Bridges tearing Brucie a new arsehole. Bridges scored two goals that day and, every time I looked round, Brucie was either rolling around on his back or flat on his stomach. That was the last game he ever played and it was a complete nightmare. You don't get many fairy-tale endings in sport.

To be fair to Brucie, nobody in a Sheffield United shirt covered themselves in glory that day. Kevin Ball, who played in midfield for Sunderland, was easily the hardest man I ever played against. He had elbows as sharp as razor blades and wasn't afraid to use them. He was a horrible bastard. He'd elbow you in the face, boot you off the ball, punch you in the back. Because I'd started the season like a train, I'd begun to make a few waves in the press. And Kevin Ball had obviously been taking note. Whenever the ball came near me, he'd say: 'Go on then, you little bastard, I dare you.' When I got the ball, he'd boot me in the air. When he shook my hand after the game, he almost snapped it off. I was still a boy and Kevin Ball was as manly as they came.

*

The Arsenal team we played against in the third round of the FA Cup was a seriously good outfit. What a side that was. They'd done the Double the previous season and I was up against Patrick Vieira in midfield that day. But there was no way I was going to be intimidated. I was playing against Bobby and Steven Brooksby on Northfield Crescent at the age of 10 and, if you dribbled past them, they'd beat you up. So Patrick Vieira didn't scare me.

That was the game that had to be replayed, after we kicked the ball out when one of our players was injured and Marc Overmars scored from the throw-in. Brucie was furious and tried to take us off the pitch, and I think Arsene Wenger was a bit embarrassed because he immediately offered us a replay. I more than held my own against Vieira and booted him up in the air a few times. He must have been thinking: 'Who is this little bastard?' In the dressing room afterwards, Brucie was buzzing at how I'd played. About two minutes into the replay, Vieira clattered me from behind. And I thought: 'That's because I ran you all over the park two weeks ago.' The one Arsenal player who did scare me was Dennis Bergkamp, but only because he was so good. He scored an unbelievable goal, a chip on the turn, and Arsenal beat us 2-1. But after those two games I thought: 'Here we go – I'm actually gonna do something.'

At this point I was still in love with football and the real, hard drinking hadn't kicked in. But I still managed to get in trouble with Brucie once or twice. One Tuesday night we ended up in The Leadmill in Sheffield. Brucie was a bit hotter on nights out than Nigel Spackman had been, which was probably down to the influence of Alex Ferguson at Old

Trafford. To get in for nothing, I offered the geezer on the door two free tickets for Saturday's game. When I went into training on Thursday, Brucie pulled me into his office.

'You've been in The Treadmill, haven't you?'

'No, gaffer.'

'You fucking have! I've had some bloke from The Treadmill ringing me up asking for those two tickets you promised him!'

'No, gaffer, that's a load of bollocks.'

'So he's lying then?'

'Yes, gaffer. Hand on heart I've never, ever been to The Treadmill in my life.'

Brucie stared at me for what seemed like half an hour.

'All right, I'm gonna trust you.'

I didn't really tell a lie, as the club wasn't called The Treadmill. The only trouble was, someone from the football club went and phoned The Leadmill. A few days later, Brucie pulled me in again and went ballistic: 'You think you're so fucking clever!' But I was like the naughty kid at school who teachers can't help liking. And Brucie seemed to like me a lot.

During a press conference after that Arsenal replay, Brucie called me 'the new Remi Moses', a reference to the former Man United midfielder. I didn't even know who Remi Moses was – I was only about eight when he retired – but Dad filled me in: 'He was a bloody good player, son.' That'll do for me. The *Sun* called me 'the new Paul Ince', and suddenly I had half the clubs in the Premier League sniffing round me. Arsenal, Aston Villa, Newcastle, Leeds – all of them were apparently interested. Sunderland had already had a £2m offer rejected on transfer deadline day – after they'd spanked us 4-0, their manager Peter Reid said it was 'Sunderland versus Curtis Woodhouse' – and Sheffield Wednesday were even mentioned. I'd rather have eaten my own shit than play for them.

But I honestly wasn't interested in playing for anyone else. I'd crawled out of all that shit that was going on back in Driffield and had come up smelling of roses. I was living the dream, representing the club I loved and playing out of my skin. Everything I'd ever wanted in life was actually happening. The fact that I could have earned more money playing elsewhere didn't come into it – I would have paid Sheffield United to play for them. And things were going so well, I was absolutely convinced I'd soon be playing for the full England team.

That season wasn't a great one for Sheffield United. We missed out on the playoffs by some distance, Steve Bruce resigned at the end of it and the club was in a bit of a financial mess. But I was flying, injury free and the best player on the pitch most weeks. I won player of the year at just 18, a record that's never likely to be broken. The fans loved me, not only because I was a rare player who'd come through the Sheffield United system, but also because I never let myself or anyone else down. I was an old-fashioned box-to-box midfielder, who could do a bit of everything. I was combative, a good leader, could score goals, tackle, defend, pass the ball. If you support a traditional working-class club and are paying hard-earned money to watch your team play every Saturday, you appreciate players like me. I was someone I'd want to sign. Maybe I should have retired then; it would have been a perfect ending.

Budapest, April 1999

I had phone calls from Jamaica before the 1998 World Cup but I turned them down because I just took for granted that I'd play for England in a World Cup one day. I'd already played for England Under-16s and Under-18s and in April 1999 I made my debut for the Under-21s against Hungary in Budapest. I didn't think it would get to me in the way it did, because it was something I'd expected to happen. But walking into that dressing room and seeing the kit all laid out, that was a really proud moment. And while I was sing-ing the national anthem, looking up at Mum and Dad in the stands (thank God there was plenty of security), I remember thinking: 'Jesus Christ, I'm actually playing for my country.' I think we all felt like that. None of us had been ruined by football yet, we were all still wide-eyed and innocent. 'Wow! Where might we all end up?'

It pissed it down that night and I played really well; they were my perfect conditions: sliding tackles, smashing into people, real muck-and-nettles stuff. We were behind 2-0 at half-time but Danny Mills and James Beattie scored after the break and it finished 2-2. All the first team were watch-ing in the stands and I remember looking up at them from time to time and thinking: 'I'll be in that team soon.' Bear in mind I was playing for the Under-21s two years ahead of schedule and was more than good enough to hold my own. But while some of the line-up that night ended up doing unbelievable things in football, I ended up getting punched in the head for a living.

A look at the subsequent careers of the lads I played with at age-group level tells you a lot about how football works. Joe Cole was unbelievable as a kid, like Lionel Messi. He was that kid in the playground who runs through everyone every time he gets the ball. David Dunne was also a great player, as was Jody Morris, but they didn't have the careers, I thought they'd have. Morris and Dunne looked far better prospects than Frank Lampard, who didn't impress me much. I didn't go back to Sheffield saying: 'Jesus, there's a player down at West Ham called Lampard who's bloody brilliant.' It was Joe and Jody I was raving about. But when you're 17 or 18, nothing's at stake. When you're 21 and playing in the Premier League, the manager's job is on the line. So all that natural talent gets coached out of them. Jamie Carragher was a strange one. He was a bit awkward on the ball, not the best passer, not the quickest. Ledley King and Jonathan Woodgate looked like better prospects. But Jamie was a natural leader, brave as a lion, and got the maximum out of the talent he had. I like players like that; they remind me of me and my boxing career.

CHAPTER 14

PROMISES, PROMISES

Dave Coldwell was a decent enough fighter, an area champion. But because he wasn't a great fighter, I think he could relate to me more than he could people like Ryan Rhodes and Kell Brook, who were groomed for stardom from a young age. It's not as if Dave saw anything special in me, but he liked that I was prepared to work. Ryan and Kell hadn't shared the same experiences as Dave coming through the ranks. Plus, Dave was badly bullied as a kid, so I think he was naturally drawn to underdogs. He loved proving the naysayers wrong and working with people who had been written off.

Dave had run one of Brendan Ingle's gyms in Sheffield, but his boxing hero wasn't Naseem Hamed, it was Johnny Nelson. Johnny lost his first three pro fights; he really struggled with his confidence but ended up a British, European and World cruiserweight champion. Even Ryan fell into the underdog category. He had been tipped for great things in the 1990s, when he went by the nickname 'Spice Boy', but after losing a world title shot in 1997 he drifted away from the limelight. When Dave took him on, Ryan was boxing six- and eight-rounders in half-empty arenas. A lot of people thought he'd retired. But Ryan ended up winning a British title again, 11 years after the first time, and eventually got a second world title shot.

So I was just about the perfect project for Dave. I never missed a day of training and I never shirked a spar. Some people who knew they were supposed to be sparring would forget their headguard or gumshield on purpose. But I never forgot mine; I jumped in every time I was asked. 'Fuck you. I'm not going to forget my gumshield so you can all laugh at me. I'm going to be there today and I'll be back tomorrow, so you can beat me up again.'

It was just like being that kid on Northfield Crescent again, when people would call me names. Like Dad used to say: 'You've got to fight them every single time they call you nigger, because nobody likes fighting every day and eventually you'll grind them down.' So I kept going back, kept jumping in with them and kept getting the shit kicked out of me. Day after day after day. Dave tells me that, in the end, people just got fed up of me being there: 'Christ almighty, he's here again, even after what I did to him last time. This geezer must have lost the plot.' But if you do that for long enough, whoever it is who's training you will eventually think: 'Hmmm, this kid might have something.' Whatever that something is, sometimes you need someone to bring it out of you, whether it be a boxing trainer, a football coach, an art teacher or whoever. A nice person who sees your passion and wants to shape it into something great. Dave was that man in my life. From day one he recognised that burning desire and knew I was going to give him absolutely everything.

Ryan and Kell were like chalk and cheese when it came to sparring. Ryan used sparring mainly as a way to hone his defence, so he'd let me attack him and not give me too much punishment back. Kell was a nasty sparrer; every time I got in the ring with him he'd try to take my head off. Sometimes Dave would step in and say to Kell: 'Listen, you're both my fighters – why am I going to put him in with you if you're going to do that to him? He's not learning anything and neither are you.'

'Sorry, Dave, I get it . . .'

Ding-ding! Exactly the same the next round. But it was good for me because the best way to learn is through a baptism of fire. I was never going to be in an actual fight situation where someone was going to tell my opponent to go easy on me. Sparring Kell was bringing me on 10-fold, because every time I went in with him I thought: 'Listen, you've got to be on your game here. Focus, otherwise you'll get a tanking.' I always got a tanking anyway; it was more a question of what level: a small tanking or a serious one. But Kell never put me down in sparring. Nobody did. I was one tough bastard.

When I first signed with Frank Warren, the idea was to fight every six weeks to build up the experience as quickly as possible – training, fighting, training, fighting. I was on

£2,500 a fight, but after I'd paid my trainer, my manager, my gym subs and for my medical and all the paraphernalia, I'd be lucky to walk away with 800 quid. So even if I hadn't had my little difference of opinion with the police in Bridlington, I would have had to go back to football at some point. I found it difficult combining boxing training with playing football. One week for a game of football I might be 11 and a half stone, two weeks later I might be 10st 4lb and absolutely knackered. It was crippling me and I kept on getting injuries. But that's just the way it had to be.

I was still miles away from completing the journey, but once I'd taken that path I couldn't turn back because my ego was involved. People were laughing at me even more after my less than impressive debut. Respected boxing writer Steve Bunce called me 'naive' and said it would be 'very difficult to turn him into a natural boxer'. Pretty much everyone was saying I wouldn't make it. But if you challenge me and tell me I can't do something, then I'll do it. My whole boxing career was a big 'fuck you' to everybody.

I moved up to light-middleweight for my second fight, seven months after the first and shortly after the British Boxing Board of Control reinstated my licence. Duncan Cottier was seriously tough; I hit him with some big shots but I just couldn't budge him. Duncan had won only two of his 28 fights but the difference between a solid, experienced fighter and someone like me was massive. He was battle-hardened; I was still a namby-pamby footballer. He outboxed me in the first round but I managed to beat him on points. It wasn't great, but a win was the main thing. I think people around me were calculating: 'Let's get him to 10-0, maybe get him a shot at an area title and that's job done.'

There was still a lot of intrigue, people wanted to come and see me – 'Roll up! Roll up for the Freak Show! Half-footballer, half-boxer!' – so I was selling a load of tickets, and presumably making money for Frank Warren, so it was in his interests for me not to get beat. If I wasn't selling tickets, it would have been a different story. The only person who wasn't making any money was me.

Rotherham, May 2007

It started out a beautiful day. I'd trained in the morning and was laid out in Rotherham city centre, listening to some music on my headphones, my bag a makeshift pillow, having a well-earned snooze. Suddenly my phone started vibrating in my pocket. It was Dad's girlfriend Julie: 'Your dad's had another stroke. This time it's a really bad one. Get to the hospital quickly.'

Dad had been fishing and fallen into the pond. The person in the next peg had dragged him out and called an ambulance. But I thought he was going to be all right. Not once did it cross my mind that he was actually going to die.

'*I'll never die, son. Dying's for everyone else. I'm a superhero.*'

I thought he'd come out like his brother Carson, maybe in a wheelchair. Then, like Carson, he'd start using a stick after a bit of rehab and be almost back to how he was. But the doctors knew different. The doctor who had done the scan took the family into a back room and told us the bleed on his brain was so big they couldn't operate on him. If they did, he'd die immediately. So we just had to sit and wait for him to pass away. But even then, I didn't think he would.

We were asked to leave the room while they cleaned his bed. But after being outside for what must have been a minute, I went back in: 'I can't leave him in there on his own.'

I sat beside him and held his hand while the nurses were going about their business. He was drifting in and out of consciousness. Suddenly, he took a couple of big breaths, opened his eyes and looked straight at me.

'Dad, I promise that I'll win the British title. I promise . . . I promise . . .'

He closed his eyes again.

'Has he died?'

'He has, son.'

I thought it only happened to other people's dads.

CHAPTER 15

ONE LONG PARTY

Glasgow, May 1999

I didn't want to leave Sheffield United, but there's not much romanticism in football. Sheffield United desperately needed money and the only way to get it was to sell their best players. So at the end of the 1998/99 season, I did a £4m deal with Glasgow Rangers. My agent, Mel Stein, had arranged for Paul Gascoigne to join Rangers a few years earlier and that had panned out pretty well, despite Gazza's madness. So on the last day of the Scottish season, I was sat next to the Rangers chairman at Ibrox watching his team parade the Premier League trophy. The next day, there was a photo of me and David Murray on the back page of the *Scottish Sun* and the caption said: 'Curt caught in the act.'

David showed me round the Blue Room, with its stacks of trophies. Someone else took me to a Versace shop and told me to buy anything I wanted. I bought one pair of black jeans. I remember thinking: 'There's nowt I want in here. I'd much rather go to Burton's, I could fill my boots in there.' After that, this father-and-son combination, who worked for the club in some capacity or other, escorted me around Glasgow. One of them said to me: 'Everyone in this town knows you've signed for Rangers. So if anyone asks you what religion you are, just say, "The same as you." Don't get into a debate or anything. It's our job to make sure you stay out of trouble . . .'

My chaperones didn't do a very good job. In their wisdom, they took me to a nightclub and I got absolutely bongoed. I brought a load of people back to my hotel room and we wrecked the place. I ran up a six-and-a-half-grand bar bill in 48 hours. As I've said, I thought the deal was done and dusted. I went back to Sheffield United, and was telling everyone how great Glasgow was, psyching myself up to say my good-byes, when I began to hear rumblings that the deal had fallen through. My chaperones must have reported back to the chairman: 'Listen, this fella's a total psychopath, run for the hills.' Rangers manager, Dick Advocaat, had a reputation as a disciplinarian so I was his worst nightmare. They'd just got rid of one nutcase in Gazza. They didn't need another one.

Wayne Quinn couldn't get away from me. I'd followed him to Tapton Mount and, when he went to live in Mosborough, I moved in with Jon Cullen just around the corner. By this stage, football was starting to get in the way of my social life. It wasn't long before me and Quinny were partying seven days a week. I wished someone had invented an eighth, just so I could fit another session in. After a game on Saturday, we'd head straight to the players' lounge and get plumbed in for the week. On Sunday morning, I'd sometimes watch my mate Andy Ward play Sunday league football, just to get some fresh air and sober up a bit, before heading to the Railway Hotel next to Bramall Lane. I might have a night off the booze on Monday but after training on Tuesday we'd all make our way down to the Pomona bar in Sheffield. I'd turn up to training dressed in my going-out gear – there wasn't a second to be wasted. Wednesday it might be all day in the British Oak in Mosborough, and eventually I started boozing on Thursdays as well. Our house was carnage, as was Quinny's. There would be people I'd never met turning up at 4am: 'In you come, grab a beer from the fridge ...' I'd wake up the next day and think: 'I've got a game in 24 hours.'

Adrian Heath replaced Steve Bruce as manager but only lasted a few months. He'd been a coach under Peter Reid at Sunderland, who had pissed the First Division title the previous season. He was a great coach and a lovely fella, but it just didn't happen for him at Sheffield United. A lot of good players had been sold, not much quality brought in, and we were right in the thick of a relegation battle by November. So Adrian was sacked and Neil Warnock replaced him.

Neil's first training session was the day before a game against Portsmouth and he had us playing 13 against 13 in this small, coned-off box. He lined us up beforehand and said: 'Anyone pulling out of a tackle will be let go by Sheffield United tomorrow.' I'm surprised no one died – there were some horrendous tackles going in. Neil was looking for players who could look after themselves and would put everything on the line for the club. That was right up my street.

Having not won since the middle of October, we won Neil's

first four games in charge. He wasn't a tactical genius by any means and didn't really coach – Kevin Blackwell did most of that. On the rare occasions Neil did take a training session, it was a disaster. You might not see him for a few days and suddenly he'd turn up on a Thursday, take a few free kicks, balloon them all over the bar, then pull the players in and have a little chat. A lot of managers struggle because they don't understand people. But Neil's strength was man management and motivation; that's where he earned his corn, especially in the dressing room on match day. He ranted and raved, but unlike Barry Fry he picked his moments, so you listened to him. Neil's a proper Yorkshire bloke, straight down the line, and he surrounded himself with good people. That's a key part of being a good manager, admitting what you're not good at. He also had a good eye for players. He brought in Michael Brown from Man City, gave academy players like Phil Jagielka their debuts and created the nucleus of a decent team. And there were still a few wrong'uns in that dressing room, so he had to have his wits about him. Like the time two of the lads – who shall remain nameless – were having a naked punch-up after a game and Neil had to come between them and break it up. The following day, one of the lads turned up to the training ground with a baseball bat in his boot.

In December, Neil made me captain for an FA Cup tie against Rushden & Diamonds. I think he sensed I was losing my hunger and that was his way of trying to get me back on track, by giving me extra responsibility. It didn't work. People always ask me: 'Can you remember the moment you fell out of love with football?' It's like asking someone to pinpoint the moment they fell out of love with a partner. It's a gradual process. I like the thrill of the chase but once I've conquered something, I lose interest very quickly. When I was 10 years old, people were telling me: 'You'll never make it as a footballer; you're too small and you're all left foot.' For years, I heard those voices, focusing on what I couldn't do. I knew there were things I wasn't good at, but I also knew I was going to prove those people wrong. I used to say: 'Listen, if your left foot was as good as mine, you wouldn't need a right foot either. If God had given me two good feet, you lot would be fucked.' So my debut against Crewe was the beginning of the end, because I'd done what I set out to do, which was to prove I was good enough. As soon as I became an established professional footballer, that was it. The more games I played, the less I enjoyed it. After a while the drive and fun evaporated. 'Wow, is this it? This can't be what I was dreaming about as a kid in Driffield?'

I look at the likes of Wayne Rooney in football and Floyd Mayweather in boxing and think: 'Fair play to you – you're from tough backgrounds but you managed to fulfil your potential while all that chaos was going off around you.' Imagine the discipline required to sustain a long career when you've got all that money, all those distractions and all those people hanging off you like leeches. Rooney isn't the player he was. But he's been playing professional football for about 15 years, has millions in the bank, a massive house and a lovely family. And he still wakes up every morning wanting to play and score goals. It takes a special personality to do that.

People go off the radar in different directions. It doesn't have to be boozing and cruising; it could be that they lose their hunger because of making too much money too soon. As Marvin Hagler once said: 'It's hard to get out of bed for your 5am run when you're wearing silk pyjamas.'

The first few months of the new century were hellish. First, I was arrested for smashing up a car and a house in Driffield after a fight in a nightclub. Quinny was out with me that night and he couldn't believe what he was seeing; it was carnage on a whole different level to anything he was used to. Then I was involved in a car crash. I was in this girl's motor I shouldn't really have been in when it got blown over by the wind. It flipped two or three times and ended up on the embankment. While I was laid out on the road, covered in blood and drifting in and out of consciousness, I could hear this girl screaming: 'Oh my God! My beautiful new car!' And I was thinking: 'I'm nearly dying here ...' I didn't suffer any serious injuries, just a few cuts and bruises. But I remember Sheffield United chairman Kevin McCabe paying me a visit. When I opened my eyes, he was standing over me with this look on his face that said: 'Please just give us one week where there are no Curtis Woodhouse stories in the papers.'

To be fair, I gave the club a few weeks off. Then I got nicked for stealing a roll of chicken wire from outside a shop and rolling it down a hill. It smashed a window but it was hardly the crime of the century. Imagine going inside for that: 'What are you in for?'

'Murder. What about you?'

'Don't you know? I'm the Driffield chicken wire thief.'

I wasn't getting my kicks from football so I was looking

for them elsewhere. If that meant nicking some chicken wire and rolling it down a hill, so be it. It was around this time that Neil pulled me into his office: 'Listen, if you carry on like this you'll be out of the game at 25. Getting nicked, boozing all the time, turning up with black eyes. I've seen better players than you end up on the scrapheap because they had no discipline. Every manager who's been at Sheffield United can't be wrong. They've all tried to put you on the straight and narrow and nothing's worked. And word gets round. Carry on like this and no one else will touch you with a barge pole.'

This was only a few months after I'd been linked with a move to Liverpool, who apparently wanted me to replace Paul Ince. Middlesbrough were also interested, as were Sunderland. So I walked out of there thinking: 'What a load of shit.' Looking back, I see that Neil Warnock was just trying to help me. At the time, I thought he was a prick. I didn't give a shit what Neil Warnock had to say. Or Adrian Heath or Steve Bruce or Nigel Spackman. They didn't know me, hadn't earned my respect, and yet they tried to dictate terms to me. I'd survived so far doing things my way. The only person I ever listened to was Russell Slade, because he knew what I'd gone through from the age of 14. Neil banned me from going back to Driffield and spoke to the press: 'If anyone sees Curtis Woodhouse out in Sheffield, let the club know.'

So I started going out in Chesterfield instead: Sheffield's loss was Zanzibar's gain.

CHAPTER 16

ME AND MY BIG MOUTH

I'd promised Dad I'd win the British title. Problem was, I didn't think I would. If his blessing had unshackled me, that promise was like attaching myself to a ball and chain. But when Dad said he was going to do something, he did it. Dad kept his promises to me, so I had to keep my promise to Dad. Or at least try to.

Dad was a hard, uncompromising man and he didn't always find it easy when events got away from him. But he was fundamentally a good human being. Bad men don't spend all their spare time and the last pennies in their pockets on making sure a son's dream comes true. Bad men don't work every hour God sends, dig so many holes that they're riddled with arthritis in their knees and elbows, to put food on the table and give their family respectability and dignity. No, Dad never hugged me or told me he loved me. But hugs and words alone are hollow. I knew he loved me and my brother and sister more than anything. He was my super-hero. And superheroes don't die at 51.

Dad's death knocked me for six and those first few weeks afterwards were probably the worst of my life; it felt like my insides had been ripped out. It's the little things that set you off. Deleting his number from my phone was horrible. Even now I sometimes think: 'I better ring Dad and tell him about this or that.' It was also the thought of the kids not getting to know him properly. He was a fantastic gran-dad, far more cuddly with Kyle and Isla than he ever was with me, and a huge personality. I wanted him to embarrass them with his dancing like he'd embarrassed me. But I had a family to feed, so I couldn't mope about for too long. It was back to boxing and back to football – my Yin and Yang.

My first fight after Dad's death was against Peter Dunn at the Barnsley Metrodome. Peter had had about 90 fights and won 11 of them. When I boxed him, he hadn't won in 30-odd contests. He was a classic journeyman, a hard-as-nails Yorkshireman who'd fight anyone, anytime, anywhere and went by the nickname 'Desperate'. In a game as dark as boxing, you've got to have a sense of humour. After the fight, which I won on points, I went public about my ambition to win the British title. Me and my big mouth – I wish I'd kept quiet. If I'd said I was going to win an area title, there would have been far less pressure on me. People would still have told me I couldn't do it, but it would have been a lot easier to prove them wrong. I let my emotions get the better of me. I was thinking of Dad. He only watched me box twice. Without him ringside, that win felt hollow.

*

My first season with Rushden was a bit stop-start. I was play-ing for them on a week-to-week contract and, after scoring a couple of goals in a handful of games, I quit in January 2007 to concentrate on boxing. But two months later, because I really needed the money, I was back again. The club were in a bit of trouble when I joined but I scored a few more goals in the run-in – including, if I say so myself, a 30-yard screamer against Northwich – and we finished mid-table. At the end of the season I bowed to the inevitable and signed a two-year deal. Still having to play football, when the only place I wanted to be was the gym, got me down. But it was like somebody who works as a waiter while they're training to be an actor – just a way of financing the dream.

While I was dreaming big, some of my early opponents were slightly less ambitious. Before my fight against Craig Tomes at Don Valley Stadium in Sheffield, I saw him lean-ing against a wall outside, smoking a fag. He looked at me and said: 'All right, mate?' And carried on smoking. I was almost offended: 'Fuck me, pal, I'm not that shit. Am I?' When I got back to the dressing room, I said to the lads: 'You'll never guess what – Craig Tomes is outside having a fag!' And nobody batted an eyelid. To them, it was perfectly normal.

Tomes was my first knockout victim. The bell went, I hit him on the chin and that was it. Big left hook, lovely shot, all over in about two minutes. I could always hit hard and if I caught somebody clean I could knock them out. But to knock somebody out you've got to be tactically and techni-cally good, create the holes to land the decisive punch. I rarely hit anybody clean in those early fights.

A knockout win was nice for my confidence but to most commentators in the media I was still a freak show. A lot of the coverage was quite patronising – 'Didn't he do well for a footballer?', that kind of thing. They didn't see me slogging my guts out in the gym, training twice as long as everyone else, finally nicking a round or two in sparring. To most people I was still this deluded bloke who was running away from football but would soon snap out of it and return with his tail between his legs. One of the few journalists who said something positive was the *Guardian*'s Don McRae. After he interviewed me, he said: 'I look forward to watching you, Curtis. I've got a sneaking feeling something special is going to happen.'

Meanwhile, I was a football writer's wet dream: 'United felled by boxer's body blow', 'Curtis vows to KO City', 'Rovers go down to Woodhouse sucker punch'. The funny thing is, the man doing most of the damage at Rushden was manager Garry Hill. I liked Garry but he was a loose cannon, like a non-league version of Barry Fry. Sometimes we'd be training and hear Garry in the background, trying to flog a white van or whatever. After I was sent off against Salisbury for booting someone, it all kicked off and Garry head-butted their assistant manager. The following Monday, the whole squad sat down to watch the video and everyone was laughing their heads off – there were fists and boots flying everywhere. I got a night in the cells and 200 hours' community service for shoving a copper; Garry got a two-week ban and a £500 fine for sticking the nut on someone. Where's the justice?

Since that episode with the coppers in Bridlington, I've

never been in trouble with the law. Boxing played a big part in that. I wouldn't say it saved me; that's a bit of an easy cliché. When I started I had a young child, 10 years of messing about as a footballer behind me, and was older and wiser. But the discipline required to be a boxer helped me consign all that other stuff to history. I couldn't go out because I was up training at five in the morning. And because I couldn't go out, I wasn't drinking. And it was when I was drunk that I'd do daft things and get myself into trouble. When I'm sober and someone wants to pick a fight with me, I can walk away, no problem – unless they're really taking liberties. But if I'd sunk a few beers and someone wanted to push my buttons, they'd get walloped. Me and alcohol hadn't mixed too well since the first time I touched the stuff, which was when I was two years old: I'd found a bottle of cheap cider in the cupboard under the sink, necked some of it and was found sleeping it off under a table. That's how we roll in Driffield.

My fight against Dave Murray was at Bramall Lane. It was a tiny venue, the same room where Sheffield United used to hold their award ceremonies and where I became the youngest-ever player of the year in 1998. It was a rowdy dinner show, packed with Sheffield United fans, and when I came into the ring to the club anthem, 'The Greasy Chip Butty Song', the place went berserk. But all I could concentrate on was the smell of the food; it was absolute agony. Mum was in the crowd that night, stuck behind a pillar. When she went to the bar to watch from there, a security guard told her to go back to her seat. Mum said to him: 'Do you know who I am?'

'No. Should I?'

'Yes. I'm Ricky Hatton's mother.'

'Oh, sorry, Mrs Hatton, stay where you are ...'

Mum didn't know anything about boxing, so it was either Ricky Hatton or Joe Calzaghe. She couldn't say me, because she was the wrong colour.

I didn't know who this Murray was either, so when I got in the ring Dave Coldwell whispered in my ear: 'When you see him, don't worry about how big he is.' He was absolutely massive, about 6ft 2in tall and wide as a bus. Because he saw I was tiny, he went straight for me and tried to take my head off. That was the difference between me and a bona fide prospect. When journeymen fight prospects, they're just looking to give the guy a decent workout and survive. But with me they'd look across the ring and think: 'I'm fucking winning this. I'm not going to let a footballer beat me at my game.' Even Peter Dunn, a guy who hadn't won in 30 fights, would have been thinking he could beat me.

So that meant every fight I had was stressful, and came with pre-fight nerves, butterflies in the pit of my stomach. And because every fight was exactly that – a fight – I was learning things and soon became battle-hardened. There wasn't much in the way of technique in the first round against Murray, but early in the second he threw a left jab, I slipped it and nailed him with a right hand over the top. It didn't last long, but it was fun while it did. And that was just how I liked it.

My dad, Bernard, and his twin brother Carson. They were abandoned by their mum, who'd come to this country from Jamaica.

Mum, little brother Karl and me on the doorstep of our house in Driffield.

With my superhero after he'd won a tug of war competition. He used to tell me he'd live forever – and I believed him.

Trophy-winner. Bridlington Rangers Under-10s – my first team, and my first taste of football glory.

I had the best season of my career in 1998/99 when I was just 18 years old, and loving playing for Sheffield United. The *Sun* called me 'the new Paul Ince'. (PA/Empics)

My form earned me a first call-up to the England Under-21s, against Hungary on 27 April 1999. Lining up alongside me that day were Gareth Barry, James Beattie and Danny Mills, among others.

(PA/Empics)

After a summer break with the team in Trinidad – when things got a little bit out of hand – my time at Sheffield United was coming to an end. I was only 20, but already trading on my reputation. (Getty Images)

Scoring my second goal at Huddersfield as Birmingham City pushed for promotion in May 2001. (PA)

Trevor Francis, who signed me for Birmingham, probably didn't expect he'd have to carry me off the pitch as well during our play-off semi-final against Preston. We lost on penalties and Trevor, a lovely bloke, was soon a dead man walking. (PA)

Challenging David Beckham at Old Trafford in the Premier League, December 2002. It should have been the pinnacle of my career, but I was drunk at the time. When I see this photo I feel nothing but disappointment.

(Getty Images)

Making my debut for Rotherham during my loan spell there in 2003 – this wasn't part of the dream. (PA)

Celebrating after scoring for Peterborough against Bournemouth in November 2003. Barry Fry had persuaded me to drop down two divisions to join them, but he couldn't rekindle my love for the game. He did, however, set me on a new path. (PA)

Battling with Stefan Moore for Hull City against QPR in November 2005. It was my final season in the Football League – within a year my life would set off in a very different direction. (PA)

Taking on 'the worst pro boxer in Britain', Dean Marcantonio (AKA 'The Mexican Window Cleaner') for my debut bout at the Grosvenor House Hotel in September 2006 – the relief when I won! (Getty Images)

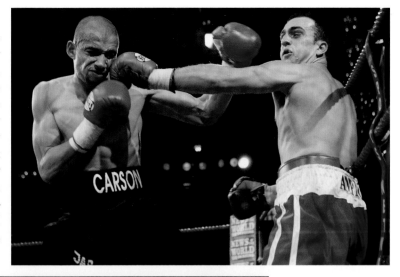

I got too confident in my fight against Peter McDonagh in October 2010, and suffered the second defeat of my career. Afterwards, I made the difficult decision to drop Dave Coldwell as my trainer.

(Getty Images)

At the weigh-in for my fight with Frankie Gavin in July 2011. The fight left me needing 14 stitches and nursing a broken rib. (PA)

You should see the other guy. Proudly showing off my English title belt after beating Dave Ryan in September 2012 – we'd thrown the kitchen sink at each other.

Getting down to 9st 9lb to fight Derry Matthews for the Commonwealth lightweight title meant I was little more than skin and bones – and in this photo I've still got 11lb to lose!

TOP: A promise kept and a dream fulfilled. Celebrating my victory over Darren Hamilton in February 2014 that meant I was British light-welterweight champion. (Mirrorpix)

LEFT: Visiting Dad's grave the day after my victory.

BELOW: My final fight? There was some repair work required after a loss to Willie Limond in June 2014, with both the Commonwealth and British titles up for grabs. (PA)

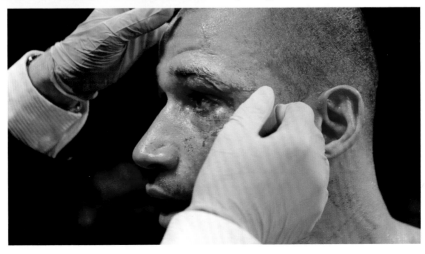

My wedding to Charlotte, with Kyle, Isla and baby Caleb all there to share the happy day.

Rediscovering my love for the game – even if it is on the beach with my boys!

Ian Ashbee and I show off my first piece of silverware as a football manager, at Hull United. I'm determined that there will be much more to follow in the future. I'd love to lead Sheffield United to the promised land of the Premier League.

CHAPTER 17

GOING ROGUE

Trinidad and Tobago, summer 2000

We didn't win a game between March and the end of the season but still managed to finish 16th, which was a minor miracle given the start we'd had. When Neil Warnock told us we were all going on a trip to Trinidad and Tobago, there was a bit of grumbling. We'd just finished a long season, so we wanted to have some of our own time. But most of us came round: 'Bit of a piss-up in the Caribbean, could be half-decent.' But when Warnock announced we weren't allowed to drink over there and that the club had organised a game against the Trinidad and Tobago national team, there was a massive uproar. People were refusing to go and Paul Devlin said to Warnock: 'I'm just letting you know: if you make me go to Trinidad and Tobago, I'm going to ruin it for everybody.'

When I got to Manchester airport at 7am, Dev had

already had a skinful. I thought to myself: 'This is gonna be complete and utter chaos.' We were on the plane for about 10 hours, which is a lot of time for drinking. Dev and Michael Brown didn't get on at the best of times. If you took a shot and it hit the crossbar, Dev would moan at you for not passing it to him. And Browny used to shoot all the time. So halfway through this flight, and about 15 bottles of vodka in, Dev and Browny started arguing. Dev, who was blind drunk, ended up attacking Browny and threatening to throw him off the plane. Warnock and the rest of the backroom staff were up the front, so they had no idea what was going on down the back. It was like a school trip, teachers on the front seats, wrong'uns on the back seats. But suddenly we heard the 'bing-bong' and the captain came on the intercom: 'If the gentleman at the rear of the plane doesn't calm down he will have to be restrained.' So now Warnock definitely knows about it.

When we landed everyone was absolutely shitfaced, but Dev was on a completely different level and still hadn't calmed down. Warnock said to him: 'Listen, Paul, now is not the time for this. We've got the president of Trinidad and Tobago waiting for us on the tarmac.' So while the rest of us had to endure this presidential reception in about 100 degrees, Dev was sent straight to the hotel in a taxi. About an hour and a half later, we walked into the hotel; Dev was stood at the bar with the taxi driver and they were both utterly bollocksed. The following morning, they put Dev on the first plane back home. He might be the only person in existence who's taken a day trip from Manchester to Trinidad.

That first morning, Warnock read us the riot act at a team meeting: 'We are here representing Sheffield United, so there will be no drinking!' Straight afterwards, Simon Tracey said to me and Quinny: 'Fancy a few snifters? You can drink as much beer as you like over here and, because it's got no chemicals, you feel fine the next morning.' Once we had the captain, Lee Sandford, on board, rounding up the others was easy: 'Listen, if we all go out together, there's not much he can do.' So we were all relaxing in this beach-front bar when Kevin Blackwell, Warnock's assistant, stormed in and started shouting:

'The gaffer wants everyone back to the hotel now!'

Sandy said: 'Fuck off, Blacky.'

Blacky said: 'What did you just say to me?'

Sandy got up and punched Blacky right in the kisser.

This was about 11.30 in the morning. We hadn't even been there 24 hours and we'd had one man sent home for being drunk and disorderly and our captain had punched the assistant manager. I felt sorry for Blacky because he probably just wanted to have a drink with us but was fed to the wolves instead. After he'd scuttled back to the hotel with blood all over his shirt, Sandy said to us: 'Right, that's it now; we've all got to stick together.' We'd all gone rogue. It was the footballing equivalent of *Apocalypse Now*.

The next day, this big Rasta drove us to the middle of nowhere so we could buy some weed, and we ended up on the beach smoking this metre-long spliff. Everyone was coughing and spluttering and completely off their tits. Me and Quinny were sharing a room and, when we got back that night, I was in the bathroom brushing my teeth when suddenly I heard Quinny screaming like a girl. When I walked in, he was standing on his bed, like that woman in the *Tom and Jerry* cartoons.

'There's a fucking massive rat in here!'

'Shut up, Quinny.'

I carried on brushing my teeth. Seconds later, this rat the size of a cat ran between my feet and I absolutely shit myself. So now there are two of us standing on Quinny's single bed and screaming at the tops of our voices. A couple of minutes later, Dennis Pettit the physio, Dean Riddle the fitness coach and Alan Gleason the kit man came bursting into the room.

'The gaffer says stop fucking about, you're waking everybody up!'

'There's a rat in here the size of a cat!'

'Where?'

Right on cue, the rat popped up again and now there were five of us on Quinny's single bed, all screaming at the tops of our voices. Suddenly, Glease jumped off the bed – he was a proper hard-core Sheffield lad – and said: 'Fuck this.' He walked over to the rat, wellied it in the face, picked it up by its tail and slung it out the window.

The next day we had a game and Warnock had the raving hump. I knocked on Simon Tracey's door that morning and he was still absolutely bongoed. This was the man who'd told us there were no chemicals in Caribbean beer and it didn't give you a hangover. The team we played against were shit and we went about 10-nil up. But just before half-time, they hit us on the counter and Simon Tracey was stood behind the goal talking to some Trinidadian girls. So at the break, Warnock went ballistic: 'You're embarrassing the football club! They've scored and you're not even in the fucking goal!'

Tracey took his gloves off, threw them on the ground and said: 'You go in fucking goal!'

It didn't end there. A few days later, me and Quinny got hold of a couple of stray cats, threw them in Dean Riddle's room and jammed his door closed. He was shouting his head off for hours. There was also a speedboat ride at about four in the morning, which could have ended in death. And the time we set one of the youngsters up with a prostitute. Only he didn't know that; he thought he'd pulled her. He was strolling around, boasting about this bit of crumpet he'd nicked, when this woman stormed up to him: 'You need to pay me!' The lunatics had taken over the asylum. But I blame Warnock for making us go. I think he knew he'd made a mistake because nobody got fined, not even Dev.

I could have played for England Under-21s at the 2000 European Championship in Slovakia. But I went to Maga-luf instead. They sounded so happy for me when they phoned to give me the good news: 'So-and-so has dropped out and you're on the reserves list – get packing!' I told them someone in my family had died and I had to go to their funeral. I was lying on the settee when they called, surrounded by women and booze. I thought: 'No chance. I've had a hard season, I'm done. I just wanna go on holiday with my mates next week. I'm not missing that for any-thing.' If my son did something like that, I'd go mental. But I just didn't care; my head was all over the place. How had it come to this? Turning down the chance to play for my country in a major tournament? Looking back, it's almost incomprehensible ...

... We were in this bar in Magaluf – or Megaruff as we called it – and it was my mate Jamie Patterson's birthday. So there's a girl with all these shots strung across her, like ammo, and I call her across and say: 'What's the most anyone's ever done?'

'Seventeen.'

'Right, Patterson wants 18.'

So Patterson's nailed 18 tequilas, one after the other, stood up and started celebrating his new record like a man possessed, punching the air and roaring his head off. Twenty minutes later, he's gone down like a felled tree. Timber!

... Back with us in Bratislava and here's England's captain, Frank Lampard ... Lampard with a low shot! Pushed away by Abbiati in the Italy goal ...

... Patterson's spewing blood and all of a sudden it's gone from party time to everyone shitting themselves and panicking. Someone rang for an ambulance and, when it turned up, this big lump picked Patterson off the floor and started slapping him and shouting in his face: 'English *bastardo*! Pissed! Pissed!' I said to this bloke: 'Listen, mate, he's spewing up blood here!' But this bloke carried on being heavy-handed. So I twatted him ...

... Francesco Coco finds space on the left ... Coco swings in a cross ... GOAL! Comandini gets in front of his marker and rises highest to head past Nicky Weaver in the England goal ... England caught napping at the back and they pay the price ...

... Suddenly it's all gone off. This big lump didn't budge

when I hit him. Another 20 or 30 people have piled in and now there are loads of coppers with dogs, lobbing tear gas. 'Time to get out of here . . .'

. . . Thompson with a cross . . . Italy fail to clear their lines . . . Jeffers! No! The Everton striker has dragged his shot wide from all of eight yards out . . .

. . . Only two people got arrested. I was one of them, the other was Rob Strickland. They drove us to the police station and chucked us in a cell. Nobody spoke any English, so nobody told us what was happening. They left the cell door slightly ajar all night, so we were shitting ourselves. We were thinking: 'Any minute now, somebody's gonna burst in and proper fill us in . . .'

. . . Ventola into the England penalty area . . . PENALTY! Carragher with a rash swing of the leg and Italy have the opportunity to double their lead . . . and it's Andrea Pirlo with the spot kick . . . Weaver sets himself . . . Pirlo makes it 2-0 to Italy, there was no stopping that . . .

. . . We were in there for two nights and nobody spoke to us. No interviews, no communication at all. Just me and Rob staring at the gap in the door. I'd been locked up a few times at home, but this was not how it normally went . . .

. . . Oh, that's lovely from Pirlo, the Reggina man with a wrong-footing backheel . . . here's Pirlo again, his movement causing all sorts of problems for England's defenders . . . Pirlo free in the area . . . great save by Weaver . . .

. . . The second morning, we could suddenly hear Lee Morris's voice in reception and it was like hearing the voice of God. 'Two of my mates have disappeared; I don't know where they are.' We started shouting: 'Mozza! Get us out of here!'

... Cort, cute ball to Jeffers, Jeffers finds Lampard, Lampard with the shot ... Abbiati denies England again and there's the final whistle, Italy have beaten England 2-0 ...

... Mozza bunged the coppers some money, so they finally let us out. But despite those two nights in a cell, I bet I had a better time in Magaluf than the England lads had in Bratislava, chasing Pirlo around for 90 minutes ...

CHAPTER 18

A BEAUTIFUL FEELING

Dad was buried with his brother Carson in Driffield. Opposite the graveyard is Driffield North End's ground, and they were the team Dad managed when I was a kid. Once when I visited there were flowers all over the grave. I stuck them in the bin. What the hell are people putting flowers on their grave for? They'd have been turning in it – Dad and Uncle Carson weren't really flower people. I don't believe in God but I do find some kind of peace at their graveside. And there are the two epitaphs to ponder: for Uncle Carson, 'Young, Gifted and Black', after the old Nina Simone song; and for Dad, 'A Stubborn Kind of Fellow', after the old Marvin Gaye song. When I end up in a box beside him, I'll save the stonemason a job, because Dad's epitaph could just as easily apply to me. And, while I didn't realise it at the time, the lyrics of that old Marvin Gaye song could have been written about my transition from football to boxing.

*

Eighteen months after joining Dave's gym and about six months after I started nicking a round here and there in sparring, I was suddenly winning more rounds than I was losing and too good to spar with people who used to beat me up. I don't think I ever took a round off Kell Brook or Ryan Rhodes, but being beaten up by them day after day, week after week, meant I was now able to do the same to other people. A torch had been passed on.

I was beginning to earn my stripes and my theory seemed to be working. My natural gift for sport combined with putting in double the work everyone else was doing meant I was finally catching up. And when my gym-mates started recognising my talent, as well as my toughness, that felt good. That's all I ever wanted – the respect of my fellow pros. I was now that boxer handing out the odd beating and wondering why they still turned up the next day: 'Blimey, I hammered him yesterday and here he is again. He must be tough as old boots.'

Birmingham, June 2008

Kell and Ryan both won British titles in 2008, which made the fire inside me even hotter. And it was no coincidence that the best performance of my career so far came on the back of their triumphs and during the football off-season, when I was able to concentrate on boxing full time. During the build-up to my fight against Wayne Downing in Birmingham, people were saying that he'd been promised an area title fight if he beat me, which pretty much everyone expected him to do. But I got him out of there in under a minute with a peach of a left hook to the body, the best shot I'd thrown in my career to that point.

I always get asked: 'What's the better feeling, scoring a goal or knocking someone out?' Knocking someone out, hands down. I know it sounds brutal but knocking someone out is so much sweeter, because you've worked so much harder for it – I trained 10 weeks for that fight. And knocking somebody out with a body shot is better than a head shot, because you get to watch them physically crumble in front of you. That's a beautiful feeling.

That win was a good guide in terms of where I was and told me I was ready to fight for an area title. When I walked into the dressing room afterwards, Frank Warren was sat there in his suit. Amir Khan–Michael Gomez was the main event so the Sky cameras were there, which made it a bit of a shop window. Frank congratulated me and said we should have a chat and get a contract sorted out. I couldn't believe my luck: 'Nice one. I'm well in here – Frank Warren wants to sign me up!' Frank had a monopoly on Sky at the time, so it seemed like a big opportunity for me. Big shows, TV exposure – what could go wrong?

Michael Gomez was a former British super-featherweight champion and my favourite British fighter of all time. So to fight on the same bill as him was a dream come true. At the weigh-in, Gomez was prowling around ready to cause trouble and I was sat in the corner like a little kid. I couldn't believe how small he was; he was tiny. Before leaving for the arena on fight night, I spotted him down in the hotel bar with his entourage, so I thought I'd go and wish him good luck:

'Michael, I just want to wish you good luck in your fight tonight.'

He took my hand, pulled me towards him and whispered in my ear: 'That cunt is gonna get bashed up.'

Gomez was as wild as they come, a man after my own heart. Acquitted of manslaughter, stabbed half to death, convicted of road rage, he made me look like Mother Teresa. For the record, Khan stopped Gomez in the fifth. But he went down swinging, which is why I liked him so much.

I ended up not signing with Frank Warren on that occasion. At the time of the offer, Dave was doing a lot of work with Hayemaker Promotions, which was run by David Haye and his trainer Adam Booth. So Dave rang Adam up, told him I'd been offered a deal by Frank Warren and asked if he could better it. I'd wanted to sign with Frank. I mean, this was Frank Warren, Britain's answer to Don King – who wouldn't want to sign with Frank? But Adam matched the deal and chucked in a signing-on fee. It also meant I would fight on Hayemaker's shows on Setanta. So it was perfect for me – regular fights and exposure on TV. But obviously Frank got the hump, because it looked as if Adam had nicked me. As with everything in boxing, it was all about ego.

My first fight for Hayemaker was a routine points win over Jimmy Beech, although Jimmy's trainer, the experienced Errol Johnson, wasn't too impressed. When Dave shook hands with him after the fight, Errol pulled him in close and whispered in his ear: 'You've got your work cut out with that kid. There's no way you're gonna keep him winning for long.' To Dave, that was like a red rag to a bull. We'd only been together for about a year and a half, but Dave understood exactly what made me tick. We talked a lot, so he was aware of the promise I'd made to Dad and exactly how determined I was to win the British title. Dave knew the light-welter and welterweight divisions ran deep, but winning that title had become as big an obsession for him as it had for me. To Dave, I'd stopped being a former footballer on some mad mission after a couple of training sessions. But not many people in the game knew me like Dave did.

The celebrations that followed my win over Jimmy Beech were far from routine, even by my standards. There were more punches landed in Liquid nightclub than there were in the ring that night. It all started when one of the bouncers pushed Dave's wife. I was standing on the edge of the dance floor next to my mate Wardy and Ryan Rhodes, who had fought on the same bill. I saw Dave, who's about 5ft 4in in heels, arguing with these bouncers and the next thing they'd grabbed his wife by the arms and lifted her off the ground. Meanwhile, Dave had been surrounded. So I slammed my drink down, ran into the middle of the dance floor and started winging punches in from all over the place. Within seconds, there must have been 40 people on the dance floor and fists were flying everywhere. It was like something out of a Wild West movie. At one point I bumped into Wardy and we started giggling like naughty schoolkids. I just loved fighting. So when the giggling stopped, I carried on punching.

The look on the bouncers' faces when Ryan strolled like John Wayne into the middle of the dance floor was priceless: 'Shit! The Spice Boy's in town!' I might be wrong, but

I think Ryan was wearing spurs on his boots that night. I had a load of mates down from Birmingham who also liked to get stuck in, so the bouncers were seriously outnumbered and we were knocking them over like skittles. We ended up throwing them out of their own nightclub and wouldn't let them back in. We took the club! Eventually someone rang the police and, when they took us outside, there were about 30 coppers with shields, dog vans, armoured vehicles, the full works. It was like the Watts riots – they had us surrounded. Loyalty can lead you down some dark and dangerous alleys.

CHAPTER 19

JUST BECAUSE

B y the start of the 2000/01 season, most of the gang had left town. From 15 of us regularly going out together, it was now me, Quinny and maybe a couple of others. And it's not quite the same when there's only four of you sat in the Chinese karaoke at two in the morning. The drinking culture had disappeared almost overnight. Suddenly, there were all these young kids and foreigners having early nights, drinking water and eating chicken and broccoli every day.

'Fancy a pint tonight?'

'Oh no, I've got training tomorrow.'

'What?!'

While I was in a pub having a pint of Guinness and eating steak and chips, everyone else was studying tactics and talking nutrition: 'This is how Arsene Wenger does things at Arsenal and this is how France do it, and they've just won the World Cup and European Championship. So we have to do it, too.' But I just thought: 'Is eating pasta really gonna make me pass the ball better?' I was a free spirit, very bullheaded. I got there doing it my way and I was fucking well going to carry on doing it my way, and damn the consequences.

The game moved on and I got left behind. I was still a big character in the dressing room; if there was anything going on, I was always smack-bang in the middle of it. And because I'd been there longer than most of my team-mates and played almost 100 games, nobody ever took me aside and told me to buck my ideas up. It was more of a joke than anything: 'Jesus, are you pissed again? Stay away from me, you stink.' In training, me and Quinny would pick the teams and always make sure we were on opposing teams, so we could mark each other. We both stank of ale, we could both barely move, so it was our little private pact.

When I rocked up on a Saturday I'd often had a week from hell and my belly would still be full of booze. Most of my team-mates were sharp, quick and strong because they'd been looking after themselves. Meanwhile, I'd been eating burgers every day and had put on loads of weight. I was supposed to be an energetic box-to-box player, someone who liked to get the tackles in, be here, there and everywhere. But that's hard to do when your belly is hanging over your shorts and you're blowing out of your arse.

My performances tailed off. The days of ripping it up and being the best player on the pitch were gone. I was only just hanging on to my place, purely on reputation. I was only 20 so it should have been easy for me to say: 'Right,

I'm changing now.' But I was old school; I had the mentality of a player from the 1980s. And I still enjoyed what I was doing, even if it was a game of dominoes and a couple of pints down the British Oak. If I heard something was going on, wherever it was, I'd have to be part of it. But I'd end up sinking 10 pints in the snooker hall, just because.

It was no coincidence that things got even worse after Russell Slade moved on. Nobody I'd known since I was an apprentice was there anymore. People used to say to me: 'Listen, the club needs you.'

'I'll try, I'll try . . .'

And I'd go straight to the pub. I was letting the club down. I should still have been their best player but I was already over the hill. And I didn't really care. The fight had gone. The light was out. It was over at the age of 20.

Me and Dad never spoke about feelings, so he didn't really know what was going on in my head. We were more like mates than father and son – we just spoke about football, birds and booze. As for my agent, I think I only met him about five times. I didn't have any interaction with Mel Stein until it was time to renegotiate a contract or sell me on. He'd be like the Invisible Man for months and then he'd suddenly ring: 'Hi, Curtis, how is everything? Sunderland are interested in signing you . . .' I felt like a commodity. But I'd be lying if I said nobody tried to help. All my managers at Sheffield United did. I remember Dad saying to me once: 'Fuckin' 'ell, son, they can't all be wankers – Adrian Heath, Steve Bruce, Neil Warnock. Have you ever thought it might be you?'

*

My personal life was also in a mess. Between the ages of 16 and 20 I had a girlfriend who was also called Charlotte, but I couldn't tell you where I met her. She was my steady girlfriend, but I had about four or five others. When I moved into the flat beneath Quinny I was still going out with Charlotte but had another girl living with me. It was hard to remember who I was with and where I was supposed to be. I soon lost respect for women. When I was in the youth team and earning £42.50 a week, a Pot Noodle and a slice of bread would suit them fine. But when I was on three grand a week, all of a sudden instead of having half a lager they'd be ordering Cristal champagne. And when I made them a Pot Noodle for dinner, they'd say: 'Really? A Pot Noodle?' And I'd be thinking: 'Hang on a minute, it's always been a Pot Noodle. What's changed?' I felt like I was being whored out and it left me feeling bitter and deflated.

It wasn't just women who wanted to fleece me. I'm not down with the cool kids, that's never been me. I'd rather be sat in a working men's club or a grotty old boozer, sinking a few pints and throwing some darts. That's where I'd feel most comfortable. People would say to me: 'What you doing drinking in here?'

'Why not? It's my local.'

'I know it is, but it's a shithole.'

If I'd gone to swanky bars more often, I wouldn't have got into so much trouble. Problem was, swanky bars are full of arseholes; they just aren't my kind of people. I couldn't think of anything worse than being in a posh bar sipping pina coladas and speaking to idiots. I'd rather be sat in the Railway Hotel speaking to Dave who works in the greengrocer's.

But trying to keep it real meant I attracted a lot of new best mates who doubled as leeches. They'd ask me for 1,500 quid for the rent or two grand for a relative's funeral. I knew they were lying but I'd give it to them anyway. People are also more likely to want to fight you down the boozer. Sheffield has two football clubs, so half the city thought I was great, the other half thought I was a wanker. Sometimes, if I'd had a particularly bad game, the whole city thought I was a wanker. Most people don't like confrontation. But I was brought up to deal with an issue as quickly as I could. So if someone started abusing me, I'd smack 'em as hard as I could, straight in the face. Just like Dad taught me. But because people soon worked out they could easily get a rise out of me, I was smacking an awful lot of them.

After the Sheffield derby, shortly before Christmas 2000, I was standing at the jukebox when loads of Wednesday fans came in and started trying to be clever. Inevitably, it all went off. Dad was with me and we both got stuck in – the superhero and his sidekick, Batman and Robin. BIF! BAM! KAPOW! It was nothing major – a few punches, a few knees, a few kicks – but I still got arrested. I was released without charge but it was all over the papers. Warnock was constantly calling me into his office, asking how I'd picked up my latest bruises and black eyes, and now he told the papers he'd slapped another pub ban on me. Then he told them: 'A couple of years ago, I thought Curtis Woodhouse was going to be a world beater.' That was his way of challenging me to knuckle down, to rediscover the old me and turn things around. But I knew my time was up at Sheffield United. I'd known it for months.

Sheffield, January 2001

I spoke to a few people and they advised me that I was in a rut and needed a change of scenery: 'Change club, get away from these mates you're drinking and partying with and it will all be fine again.' One day after training, Warnock pulled me in and told me Birmingham City had put in a bid for me.

'You can go to Birmingham or we can offer you a new three-year deal.'

'I'll go and speak to Birmingham.'

It was over as quickly as that. I'd been at Sheffield United since I was 16, was in the first team at 17, was their youngest-ever player of the year and captain. But within 90 minutes of that conversation with Warnock, I was gone. I didn't even get the chance to say goodbye to Mary and Sue in the laundry room. I didn't say goodbye to anyone. I jumped in the shower, got in the car and drove down to Birmingham. I had so much affection for Sheffield United but it was a relief it was over. I didn't want my career unravelling there, the club deserved better: 'It's not you, love, it's me.' I thought it was for the best that I go and unravel somewhere else instead.

CHAPTER 20

THE PENNY DROPS

Mansfield, 2009

In January 2009, I signed for Mansfield. From playing against Liverpool at Anfield seven years earlier, I was now involved in a relegation scrap in the Blue Square Premier. David 'Reg' Holdsworth had just been appointed Mansfield's manager and I was the first person he called. Having played with Reg at Sheffield United and Birmingham, he knew I was just the man for the job, to the extent that he was willing to make me the best-paid player at the club. And that was a trend that repeated itself throughout my football career: Peter Taylor had worked with me in the England Under-21s before signing me for Hull; Colin Hill had seen what I'd done at Peterborough before bringing me to Rushden; Russell Slade knew exactly what I could do when he signed me for Grimsby. Even after the love had gone and I was just playing for the money, I could still play a bit. And every time I crossed the line, I always gave 100 per cent, even when my body wouldn't allow me to do what I used to be able to do.

Reg knew the club needed some spirit injected, a complete identity change. Our left back was what you might call a little bit semi-skimmed, so against Wrexham away Reg brought me on and I immediately almost got sent off for a silly tackle. He had to take me off and, as I walked past him, he gave me this horrible stare. But that was all Reg needed to do. I knew I'd let him down and he knew I just wanted to win so badly, especially for an old mate.

My first defeat gave me the first inkling that the boxing community didn't really want me in their club. It was a six-rounder against a kid called Jay Morris in Belfast and the referee awarded it to him by a point. The Setanta pundits all had me winning the fight by two rounds. In fact, just about everybody in the Ulster Hall thought I'd won it. But there it was in black and white, the first 'L' on my record. That decision seemed like a disaster and left a horrible taste in my mouth. I've always been a terrible loser, even when I was a kid. When I played Monopoly against Mum and she had to nip to the toilet, I'd be a millionaire by the time she came back. Then when she questioned how, the board and all the pieces would end up in four corners of the room. My brother Karl was completely different. One sports day, he was winning the sack race when this little lad next to him tripped up. Karl stopped to help him up and they finished joint last. Dad was yelling at him: 'You could have had that!'

'But I won a lolly!'

'Who cares about a lolly?!'

To me, it was always about winning. Second was no good. If it had been me in that sack race, I would have trampled all over that little lad's back. So on the plane back from Belfast I felt like quitting. I said to Dave: 'I'm not sure I can do this anymore. If I can't beat Jay Morris, I've got no chance of achieving anything.'

There was still a lot of talk in the papers and on internet message boards about my rawness and lack of amateur pedigree, and I was starting to believe what I was reading. But Dave soon snapped me out of it: 'Keep going, Curtis. If you don't, you'll look back and regret it. I will get you a shot at the title, I promise ...'

Dave thought I'd won the bout, but he also knew I was flat that night and tanked down the stretch. I'd taken a pummelling on the ropes, hadn't really known how to fight myself out of a tight spot. But it was that defeat that made me realise that losses in boxing are big slugs of medicine that make you stronger.

When I decided to leave Mansfield for Harrogate Town, my fall through the leagues continued. I'd done the job Reg Holdsworth brought me in to do at Field Mill, helping to keep them up, and now it was all about me and my boxing career. Training full time, playing twice a week and trying to fit in enough time in the gym was killing me physically and mentally. Some games for Mansfield I had absolutely nothing in the tank because I hadn't eaten anything for a week. That combined with the fact that I didn't really want to be there meant I was a shell of the player I was, miles away from being the best player on the pitch. Harrogate were in the Blue Square North and playing for them meant I didn't have to train and could just turn up on match day. They also paid me ridiculous amounts of money, which must have put a few noses out of joint. But that was one of the upsides of being a professional boxer – nobody was going to say anything to my face. Harrogate was also nearer to Dave's gym in Rotherham, so I was never out of there, still doing twice as much work as everybody else.

After my first loss, I was out of the ring for seven months. I was supposed to fight Hull's Glen Matsell at the KC Stadium but he pulled out and the show was cancelled. I was a small welterweight – I'd be coming into the ring at 10st 10lb and my opponents would be 11st 6lb – and Dave was having trouble matching me at 147, so we decided it would be best if I dropped down to 140. My first fight at light-welterweight, my first fight in Hull and my first fight topping the bill was against Dean Hickman at the Gemtec Arena. Dean was a former Midlands Area champion, had fought for the English title twice and had wins over the then English welterweight and Commonwealth lightweight champions on his record. During the build-up to that fight I really felt some extra pressure. I'd sold a lot of tickets locally, and was expecting a lot of friends and family in the crowd, so I didn't just want to win, I really wanted to put on a show. I knew being involved in ding-dongs was good for publicity and ticket sales, but I genuinely enjoyed it. Luckily for me, so did Dean Hickman.

I predicted I'd knock Hickman out in four rounds. It took me six, but it was still a bit of an upset in most people's eyes. The difference between that fight and my loss against Morris was experience. Hickman had a big ego, considered himself a genuine prospect, and fully expected to win. But I controlled the fight with my jab, outboxed him, withstood some big punches and eventually overpowered him. It was my best performance so far by some distance and the moment Dave really began to believe that something big was in the offing. Even the press started writing a few nice things about me.

A few months after beating Hickman, I got my revenge over Jay Morris at the Magna Centre in Rotherham, which soon became like a second home to me. Because I was able to concentrate almost completely on boxing during the build-up, I was in far better nick physically, technically and mentally. Dave had sparring partners laying into me on the ropes and I started learning how to pick my shots and land with counters. I was no longer a sitting duck. I kicked off that fight like a train and almost knocked him out in the opening round. But I made no mistake in the third, flooring him with a big right cross. The same right cross I'd been working on for the past three years ... right hand, turn it over, right hand, turn it over, right hand, turn it over ... I must have thrown that shot a million times in Dave's gym and – BOOM! – at last the penny had dropped.

The day after that fight, I was in Mum's pub having a few drinks when this geezer walked in and started eyeing up my new belt. The International Masters title isn't worth a carrot and the belt is one of the ugliest things you've ever seen – it looks like it's made out of cardboard. But a belt's a belt. Anyway, this geezer finally wandered over to my table and said: 'I see you won last night. Can I be rude and ask how much you got paid? Let me guess . . . 200?'

'Two hundred what?'

'Two hundred grand?'

I started laughing.

'Mate, you're miles off.'

'What? You got more than 200 grand?!'

I got two and a half grand for that fight. Just like I got two and a half grand for most of my fights. And I only had three of them in 2009, four in 2010. For seven of the eight years of my boxing career, I was on less than the minimum wage – miles less – and I had a wife and kids to support. And my trainer and manager were only taking 15 per cent, instead of the 25 per cent they were entitled to. People see a belt around your waist and think you must be pulling in millions. But only a lucky few make a decent living from boxing. That geezer in Mum's pub thought I was sleeping in a bed covered in bank notes, like Floyd Mayweather. But while Mayweather was Manchester United, I had more in common with Harrogate Town. Not much glamour at Wetherby Road . . .

CHAPTER 21

DIDN'T LIKE IT ANYWAY

Birmingham, February 2001

F unny how different relationships come to an end. You might be with a woman for only a few months and you'll be smashing the place up when it finishes. I guess that happens when the fire inside is still burning. Sheffield United was the love of my life, the club that saved me. I used to think I was going to be at Sheffield United forever. Yet when we parted ways, as they say in the papers, there was no kicking or screaming. A cold conversation – 'Stay if you like, I don't really care' – a shake of the hand, out the door, in the car, heading towards a club I knew I could never love. Heading towards oblivion.

I didn't meet Trevor Francis before he signed me. I didn't even have a medical. The word of Reg Holdsworth, who had joined Birmingham from Sheffield United the previous season, was apparently enough for him. Reg knew what I could do when I was on my game and I was still only 20. They were both thinking I had 15 years left in football. I'm pretty sure I would have passed a medical anyway. It's not as if they could see inside my mind.

After I signed, Trevor was raving to the papers about me. After my debut against Norwich, he was raving about me even more. I only met up with the rest of the team a couple of hours before kick-off but I played a blinder and we won 2-1. Trevor made a comment afterwards about my team-mates struggling to keep up with me. And I was all smiles for the cameras. But that evening, I saw that big, shiny red button again . . .

'Whatever you do, do not press that big, shiny red button over there . . . I wonder what that button does?'

Nag, nag, nag . . . I pressed it in the end. Birmingham had put me up in the Hilton while I looked for a house, so I was sat on my bed in my hotel room, staring at nothing in particular on TV, when the phone rang: 'Hiya, Curtis. It's Trevor Francis. What are you up to tonight?'

'Nowt, gaffer.'

'I was thinking maybe I'd come up to the Hilton with my wife, have a glass of champagne to celebrate your debut?'

'I don't drink champagne but I'll have a drink with you, gaffer . . .'

A few hours later, there I was with Trevor and his wife, feeling about as uncomfortable as I'd felt in my life. So I thought: 'I'm gonna get shitfaced, just to get rid of the nerves.'

Trevor is a lovely man and his wife is a lovely lady. They're just not people I'd choose to drink with. I must have put away five pints. I spent more time at the bar than I did at the table. When I was at the table, I was swearing my head off and spilling beer. After the fourth or fifth pint I could tell Trevor was looking at me and thinking: 'What on earth have I signed here? I spent £1m on this bloke.' After about an hour, Trevor said: 'I think we'll leave you to it . . .' When they left, I was sat at the bar, absolutely bongoed, thinking: 'Did that just happen? Five hours ago, I was playing out of my skin on my debut and the gaffer was praising me to high heaven.' And I swear, in the distance, echoing all the way down the M1, I heard the uncontrollable laughter of Neil Warnock.

Cardiff, February 2001

From the age of 12 years old, I'd only ever played in red. So playing against Sheffield United in my second game for Birmingham was weird. The away changing room didn't spook me; I'd been in there loads of times as an apprentice, squeegeeing the place out on my hands and knees. But the standing ovation in the ground when my name was announced really got me. It made me feel like I was still one of them, or at least should have been. Every time I got the ball I wanted to pass it to a red-and-white shirt. To make things worse, we – by which I mean Birmingham – got walloped 3-1. Suddenly, that standing ovation was a distant memory:

'WOODHOUSE, WHAT'S THE SCORE? WOOD-HOUSE, WOODHOUSE, WHAT'S THE SCORE?'

That stung.

A few weeks after joining Birmingham we played Liverpool in the League Cup final in Cardiff. Because I'd already played for Sheffield United in that year's competition, I was cup-tied. So instead of sticking a suit on and watching the game at the Millennium Stadium with the club officials, I rounded up a few mates and went on the piss all day in the city centre. I didn't even know what the score was until the next day. You don't get *Match of the Day* when you're banged up in a cell . . .

. . . I seem to remember we got wrecked and ended up in a curry house. I seem to remember there was a disagreement over the bill between my mate and the waiter . . .

'Nobody was drinking Diet Coke on this table.'

'Just pay your bill and get out.'

When you're pissed, you don't realise how loud you're being.

'We'll leave when we're ready.'

All of a sudden, the manager came flying out of the kitchen like a bat out of hell . . .

'You pay for your Coke! You pay for your Coke!'

My mate Paul was about six-foot-four. But before he was even out of his chair, the manager, who must have been about 70, hit him with the old one-two. He was pretty tasty, with a decent technique. So at this point I'm laughing my head off, because my giant mate's just been chinned by an old geezer. But when he got up, the waiter hit him over the head with a chair. Now it's not so funny. My mate is ironed out on the floor with blood pouring out of his head and there are about 10 waiters up against me and my other mate Ross, who can't fight to save his life. I thought: 'If you want a chair fight, I'll give you a chair fight.' So I picked one up and started swinging it round my head like Tarzan. It was like the OK Corral again. Except in a curry house in Cardiff. Over a Diet Coke. I was on a lot of money at the time. Ridiculous. Looking back the whole thing was embarrassing. My mate Paul ended up unconscious with a fractured skull, the place got wrecked, and the other people in there must have been shitting themselves. But at the time I couldn't give a shit. By the way, Liverpool beat us on penalties. Another day to forget.

I told Trevor I'd just been involved in a bit of a scuffle. He didn't need to know the details, although obviously word leaked out. But no one warned me about my behaviour. No one shouted at me. In fact, I spoke to Karren Brady, who was the managing director, just once between the day I signed and the day I left. As long as I was an asset to the football club, I could pretty much do what I wanted. Even smash up an Indian restaurant. It's only when you stop being an asset that clubs start to flex their muscles.

When I first moved to Birmingham, I didn't know anyone. But Reg Holdsworth was in the process of moving house, so he soon joined me in the Hilton. Not long after that Danny Sonner, another old partner in crime from his Sheffield Wednesday days and a man who makes me look like the saint of saints, also pitched up. Jamie Pollock, who can drink like a fish, soon completed the set. I'd not been in Birmingham a week before I was in a heavier drinking club than in Sheffield. We'd finish training, head back to the hotel and sit in the bar all day, courtesy of Birmingham City.

Because Karren Brady was paying for everything, we got pissed all day, every day. And there were a lot of fit women in the Hilton, so we were going through them like skittles. I was meant to move out after eight weeks but I was still in there after five months, when Brady finally rang me and told me I had to get out. So Dad went online and bought me a big house on a golf course in Solihull. I hadn't even seen it before I moved in.

I had no idea how to run a house on my own so I asked my brother to move in with me. Unfortunately, he wasn't much better. Reg was a little bit more worldly, shall we say, so he'd offer to do a bit of cooking and take us out shopping. The first time we were in Waitrose, he was filling his trolley with chicken and fish and fruit and vegetables and, when he turned round, he saw me with a basket full of Pot Noodles. He couldn't believe it – I was a professional footballer with plenty of money, eating like a student. But I honestly thought they were good for me; I didn't know any better.

Another time, Reg took us to a Japanese restaurant. Japanese wasn't really my thing. It got to about three in the afternoon, when a waiter tapped Reg on the shoulder: 'Excuse me, sir, your friend has been taken outside ...' Because I hadn't eaten anything, I was all over the place. So Reg took me to buy some chips and sat me on a wall. When he came out of the chippy, I'd disappeared. I'd fallen into a thorn bush in someone's front garden. That morning, I'd bought a £700 Armani leather jacket. It was completely shredded. Reg tells me I climbed out of this thorn bush, threw off the jacket and said: 'I didn't like it anyway ...' More money, more problems. Bang goes the new start.

CHAPTER 22

CHEQUE MATE

Look at my boxing record and every one of those wins could quite easily have been losses. Dave used to say to me: 'You can beat anyone out there on your day. Problem is, anyone out there can beat you.' Even after I quit football to concentrate on boxing full time, my form was all over the place; I was just so erratic. There were no gimmes for me; I had to be at my absolute maximum to compete. But the morning after I beat Stefy Bull, I thought to myself: 'You know what, I was good last night. I might be able to keep this promise, after all.'

Bull had won an area title, fought for the English title and been in with Amir Khan. The fight before me he'd knocked out Dean Hickman in two rounds. He had real credibility in the game. Not only did I beat him, I took him apart in his own backyard. That fight was also live on Sky, so as well as proving that I could deal with all sorts of stresses, it made me more marketable. Sky commentator Adam Smith called it 'an undercard classic'. Also ringside that night was Frankie Gavin. Frankie was Britain's first ever amateur world champion and earmarked for great things. He was Frank Warren's golden goose and the plan was for me to be his next sacrificial lamb. Unfortunately, I knackered my hand and the fight, which was meant to have taken place 10 weeks later, was canned.

My next outing was scheduled to be against Jason Cook, who had fought for the British title twice, but he pulled out late. Instead, I was matched with Peter McDonagh, who had lost six of his previous eight fights and was heading down the journeyman route. Meanwhile, I'd signed with Warren because Hayemaker had lost their TV deal when Setanta went tits up. Obviously, what with things going so well, McDonagh beat me. I boxed well for the first few rounds, was pissing it, but I started loading up, lost my rhythm and he ended up fiddling me out of it on points. A couple of days later, I rang Dave and told him I'd decided to find a new trainer. Dave was devastated. We'd been together for three years, through thick and thin. Mostly thin. He'd recognised the passion, had faith in my potential and realised the promise I'd made to Dad might actually happen. And now I was leaving him. The old promoter Mickey Duff had it spot-on: 'If you want loyalty, get a dog.' When young footballers or boxers ask me for advice, I always say: 'Be selfish.'

I owed Dave so much. He'd invested so much time and emotion in the project, even though I wasn't making him much money. He didn't have any TV, was getting by on ticket sales and sponsorship, and was only making about

£400 every time I fought – a pittance when you consider how many hours he was putting in. But because he was doing more and more work for Hayemaker Promotions to earn a few quid, he wasn't able to give me 100 per cent. So it didn't matter that he'd taught me almost everything I knew, I had to walk away. It wasn't easy, believe me. But nothing is in boxing.

Losing a fight is not like losing a football match. When you lose a football match you get over it pretty quickly, because you might have a chance to make amends a few days later. When you lose a fight, it's a crushing feeling, like a little bit of your manhood has been stripped away. And the worst part is, you might have to wait months before you get an opportunity to erase the memory. It felt like my world had ended when I lost to Peter McDonagh. I moped about the house and ate about five tubs of ice cream in a week. I was like a male version of Bridget Jones, wallowing in self-pity.

The man I asked to make it all better was Glyn Rhodes, who had a gym in Sheffield. But now the problem was getting fights. Under Frank Warren, I had hoped to be fighting five or six times a year but I wasn't getting on his shows. It seemed like I'd been written off. And because I was still contracted to him, I was effectively unemployed and unemployable. So my first fight after losing to McDonagh was on one of Dave's shows in Rotherham. Dave had stopped being my trainer, but he was still my manager, having long since taken over from Dean Powell. And even though I'd left his gym, he was still a mate and determined to get me that British title shot. Thank God. What were Frank Warren or Eddie Hearn going to do with a bloke who was losing to journeymen? Nothing. But Dave never stopped believing.

Six months after losing to McDonagh, I knocked out Billy Smith in two rounds. Redemption and relief. A few weeks later, I was told my next fight would be against Frankie Gavin. Because Frankie is from Birmingham and I used to play for them, the press conference was mobbed. This one reporter asked me: 'Curtis, how do you see the fight going?'

'I think I can grind him down and knock him out late on.'

This reporter started laughing. A proper belly laugh. Then he said:

'Can you even spell "knockout"?'

So now the whole room is laughing. Not only am I deluded, I'm thick. It made my blood boil. I wanted to chin that silly little bastard, a so-called boxing expert who had probably never set foot in a ring. I'd had the balls to chase a dream and fight a former world amateur champion in his own backyard and here I was being disrespected. Even Frankie joined in. He called me an idiot and mocked my football career. One line he came out with was actually quite funny: 'I hardly ever saw him when he played for Birmingham because I only watched the first team.' But all this ridicule was the best thing that could have happened. It lit a fire under me, transported me right back to Northfield Crescent ...

'Barnes collects the ball on the halfway line ...'

'You're not gonna score this time ...'

'Barnes nutmegs one, lays it off to Beardsley ...'

'You're not gonna make me look like a mug ...'

'Beardsley to Barnes, who leaves another on his backside ...'

'Somebody stop him!'
'BARNES PROVES THEM ALL WRONG!'
'NOT AGAIN!'

Almost everyone thought I was shit and was going to get battered. But I didn't believe what I was hearing – I preferred to believe my own eyes. Yes, Frankie was a former world champion but I'd watched him fight in the pro ranks and didn't think he was that good. He certainly wasn't the second coming of Sugar Ray Leonard that Warren was making him out to be. He had good feet, fast hands but couldn't punch. I was confident I could give him a fight and that it wouldn't be the one-way massacre everyone was predicting. I never trained so hard for a fight in my life, and got into unbelievable shape. I was something like 100-1 to win, but I thought: 'Am I really that bad?!' So I stuck a good few quid on me winning by split decision. Every sportsman has one night when they know they're going to perform out of their skin. And I knew this was going to be that night.

Because me and Frankie were kind of in between light-welter and welterweight, the fight was made at 10st 3lb. But during the build-up, I got a phone call: 'Frankie can't make 10st 3, can you do 10st 5?' That suited me perfectly. I wasn't a light-welterweight anyway, while he probably should have been fighting at lightweight. He wasn't stronger than me; he was a speed fighter and I was a power fighter. So the higher we went, the better it was for me, not only because I got stronger and he got slower, but also because I demanded a grand for every extra pound. I was originally getting paid 10 grand, which was four times my previous biggest pay day. But I knew it was going to be a tough fight, so I wanted to squeeze every last drop out of them. A week later, I got another phone call: 'Frankie can't do 10st 5, can you do 10st 7?' Again, perfect. I was absolutely delighted. I felt like phoning Frankie up and saying: 'Go as high as you like, pal. Wanna make it at cruiserweight?!'

At this point in my boxing career, my football earnings had dwindled and the money I was getting for my fights wasn't even covering my training costs. So now that I had 14 grand coming my way, I booked a holiday for all the family. My kids are active, so is the missus, so I thought Center Parcs would be ideal. The kids hadn't had a proper holiday for years, so you can imagine how excited they were. It made me feel like a proper dad, providing for his family.

Birmingham, July 2011

I gave Frankie a fight all right. When the bell rang, the truth came out. As the rounds ticked by, I was thinking: 'Still think this is a joke fight? Still think you're levels above me? Still think you're gonna beat me easily? I bet you don't. Get ready, there's more to come. FUCK EVERYONE!' I left him covered in blood, punched the disrespect out of him. I even outjabbed him at times, won some of the boxing battles. A lot of people thought I'd won the fight, including me. If I'd been the home fighter, I would have. While I was waiting for the decision, I was thinking: 'Jesus, I could make a fortune here.' But the split decision went to Frankie.

When I watched it back, I had to admit he'd nicked it. I didn't know enough to cut off the ring; his feet were too good, and I let him sneak rounds off me. He was just too experienced, while I'd only boxed one southpaw before. And nobody's a southpaw in a pub or a car park. I'd lost no face, left my mark and learnt a lot. And I was happy to have gained the respect of the boxing world at last. At the same time, I was annoyed by the reaction of those around me. I was crying in the dressing room, but everyone else was celebrating as if I'd just won a world title. Ryan Rhodes and Kell Brook came in and said: 'Why are you upset? You boxed great.' But that wasn't what I was about, and it suggested that they didn't know what I was about, either. I didn't take the fight to box great; I took the fight to win. I knew I'd win a British title if I got the opportunity – I had blind faith. So I found their reaction patronising. It was like being patted on the head and told: 'Didn't you do well, lad? Especially for a footballer.' I felt like saying: 'Do you lot know I actually lost?'

Later, me and Frankie were sat next to each other getting stitched back together – he had eight, I had 14 – when he said to me: 'I wasn't expecting you to be that good. That was the hardest fight I've had, amateur or pro.' That was nice of him, after everything that had been said. And it restored some pride – pride that at least I'd given everything for the cause. As well as 14 stitches – six inside my mouth, six in one eye, two in the other – I'd separated a rib. I was pissing blood for four days, from all the body shots he'd hit with me. And what was my reward? A cancelled holiday.

Unfortunately, the money for the fight didn't come through as quickly as I'd hoped. When I phoned up Dean Powell he offered to do what he could to help speed up the payment.

Dean, who has since sadly passed away, was a lovely bloke. But, sat at home nursing a broken rib and pissing blood, I was getting angrier and angrier as the days ticked by.

Luckily I'd kept some ticket money to get me by, but I had to ring the travel agent to cancel the holiday. Then I had to sit Charlotte and the kids down and tell them: 'I'm sorry, we can't go on holiday now, Daddy's got no money.' I felt like the world's worst dad, a piece of shit. They'd been looking forward to it so much. That shattered me. Of course, I got the money in the end, but by then I was ready to go into another fight, so we couldn't re-arrange our holiday.

CHAPTER 23

SOMEBODY BLOW THE WHISTLE!

Birmingham, May 2001

Despite combining it with the equivalent of a five-month stag do, including that embarrassing incident in the curry house, my first half-season with Birmingham was a success on the pitch. Even when the side was decimated by injuries and hit the skids down the stretch – at one point losing six in seven – I was still being praised for my efforts in the local papers. And on the last day of the season against Huddersfield I scored my first two goals for the club – the second a good, old-fashioned diving header – as we made sure of a place in the playoffs.

Trevor Francis said some very nice things about me, including this snippet in the *Birmingham Post*: 'He has a strong competitive edge; he works exceptionally hard and has a lot of natural ability on the ball. If he's only 21 now, you can imagine how good a player he's going to be in a couple of years.' Trevor thought we'd be working together in the Premier League the following season and I'd be one of his most trusted soldiers. But professional football is like that old Sinatra song, 'That's Life': 'Riding high in April, shot down in May.' The big difference being, me and Trevor never got back on top again.

We won the first leg of the playoff semi-final against Preston 1-0, with me pressed into action at left back. But the second leg at Deepdale turned into a bit of a nightmare. We were leading 2-1 on aggregate until a last-gasp goal by Mark Rankine took the game into extra time. Apparently Trevor had been promised that if it went to penalties, they'd be taken at the end that had just been demolished. But when the time came, the referee wanted them taken at the other end, where all the Preston fans were. Trevor lost it and ordered us off the pitch. But he didn't get his way in the end. Trevor was true Blue, a Birmingham legend, and his club had been in the wilderness for years. I think the pressure was finally starting to show. I'm not sure whether our players were spooked, but Marcelo and Darren Purse missed their penalties and, when Paul McKenna scored his, Preston were on their way to Cardiff instead of us. I didn't fancy taking a penalty that night. And because others had missed and we'd lost, I felt like I'd left my destiny in other people's hands. After that, wherever I went, I always volunteered to take one. At least then if I got knocked out, it was down to me.

After that semi-final, I went out and got hammered with Reg Holdsworth. Trevor probably went home and cried.

*

We made a pretty poor start to the 2001/02 league season, but the result that really did for Trevor was a 6-0 mangling by Man City in the third round of the League Cup. Darren Huckerby scored four and, quite honestly, we were appalling. We let Trevor down badly that day. When the poor bloke was given a vote of confidence by Karren Brady, we all knew he was a dead man walking. Footballers always look for an excuse as to why things aren't going right – it's never our fault. So we knew that as soon as we had a bad run, they'd start sharpening the axe. It didn't matter how much Trevor loved the football club. A few days after that gubbing at Maine Road, we beat Barnsley 3-1. When Trevor left the dressing room that night, he said to us: 'See you all on Monday.' He did see us on Monday, but only to say goodbye for good.

On the Sunday, he'd been pulled in by Brady and co-chairman David Gold and told he was being sacked 'by mutual consent'. I'll never forget the look on his face when he sat us all down to tell us he was on his way. That look will haunt me forever; it was horrible seeing him like that. He was a man betrayed, heartbroken, had tears rolling down his face. He loved Birmingham City like I loved Sheffield United. I made my debut for Sheffield United at 17, but Trevor first played for Birmingham at 16 and made 300 appearances for the club. He was still a brilliant player when he was manager; he just couldn't run anymore. He was also a really nice man. Maybe too nice – he didn't have a shout in him. And because he was so nice, he surrounded himself with nice people – Mick Mills, Ian Bowyer – and nobody was scared of any of them.

Most players don't give two shits about clubs; they play for people, not the badge on their chest. We had a bloody good squad but people took the piss. People like me. I was partly responsible for Trevor's downfall. I gave my all for him on match day; my ego never allowed me not to try. But better preparation allows you to try even more and I wasn't in any kind of shape. He deserved 100 per cent from me and I maybe only gave him 50. Even though I was trying my best, my best just wasn't very good. Those balls I used to be able to get to, those tackles I used to be able to put in, those runs I used to be able to make, I couldn't do it anymore. Trevor's sacking was a great lesson in management: your great passion, the thing that consumes you and keeps you awake at night, might mean very little to your players. And there's not much you can do about it.

David Gold seemed like a decent bloke. He always took the time to speak to you and was always respectful and polite. It was David Sullivan, Birmingham's other co-chairman, I had a problem with. He was one of those chairmen who'd storm into the dressing room after a game and start berating the players, even though he knows little about football. He's not the worst, but I still think he's a weasel. But some of the things David Gold said after Trevor was sacked were also below the belt. The papers reported him calling Trevor a 'spoilt boy' and 'a jinx'. Saying that, he might have been right about the jinx bit. Under Trevor, Birmingham had reached three playoff semi-finals and lost them all, as well as a League Cup final. Birmingham were a big club and had a great set of proper, diehard fans, but they hadn't been in the top tier since the mid-1980s. So Gold and Brady's frustrations were understandable.

The day after Trevor was binned, I read in a paper that Steve Bruce was being lined up as our new manager. I remember thinking: 'I'd better start looking for a new club.' A few weeks passed before the official announcement was made. Bruce had only been at Crystal Palace for half a season, Wigan for a couple of months before that, and had developed a reputation for being a bit flaky. But he obviously saw plenty of potential at Birmingham and maybe even liked the idea of linking up with a few old faces from his Sheffield United days. He would have recognised my face when he turned up, but not the player.

The end of my time at Sheffield United and the start of my career at Birmingham all blurs into one. I could have been anywhere. Having more money just meant I could go out even longer. When you're someone on an average wage, you have to go home at some point because you'll run out of money. When you're a professional footballer you can stay out forever – although sometimes I'd go out with five grand in my pocket and have to borrow a tenner for a taxi home, because I'd spunked it all on champagne and gambling. I'd wake up in the morning and, because I felt so awful from the night before, I'd have a can of Stella before I trained, as a livener. I'd gone from being a social drinker to drinking really heavily and I didn't know why I was doing it. I suppose it just became a habit. Some people have a bacon sarnie for breakfast; I'd have a can of Stella. My fighting weight at Sheffield United was 11st. By the time Bruce was appointed at Birmingham, I was about two stone heavier. I had proper tits and a belly. Managers notice things like that.

Bruce's first game in charge of Birmingham was away at Wolves, and we lost 2-1. In the dressing room afterwards, he basically said the result was all my fault and we ended up having this big slanging match. I hadn't done anything in particular; I just hadn't played very well. And I'd played a lot worse than that. I think because he knew me, he decided I'd be a good person to shout and scream at, to show that he had muscles and was not to be messed with. Bruce's arrival at the club was the beginning of the end of my time there. He was looking to clear players out and he probably thought: 'This fat kid Woodhouse is top of the list.'

We fell out a lot, really didn't get on. I'd rip my bib off on the training ground, tell him to fuck himself and storm off. He must have been as frustrated as me: 'What the hell has happened to that promising kid I had at Sheffield United?' Against Millwall at The Den, I came on as a sub and got sent off after a minute for a two-footed tackle. I had the raving hump I wasn't playing in the first place and thought: 'Someone's having it here.' That was the match where one linesman got hit with a meat pie, the other got pelted with bottles, and Bruce and Mark McGhee, his opposite number, got sent to the stands for going mental at the referee. When I was given my marching orders, the Millwall fans were frothing at the mouth. I started walking off the pitch, then started walking a little bit quicker, and eventually I was almost sprinting down the tunnel. When Bruce finally collared me, he gave me both barrels again. He was at his wits' end.

But his biggest problem was that I still had four years left on my contract. I had a chance to move to Crystal Palace, where Trevor Francis had ended up, but I thought: 'Birming-ham is a bigger city than Sheffield, with more places to go out and more fun to be had, so I can't go to London. London might kill me.' Even while I was spiralling out of control, I still had that self-awareness. When you're a professional footballer, no doors are closed. I'm the sort of person who will walk through all of them. And London has more doors than any other city.

Liverpool, January 2002

Every time the ball gets humped I stare up at the Anfield lights and feel dizzy. When I look away the stars stay with me. Steven Gerrard is everywhere. It's like there are five of him. And they're all machines. They're running fuck-ing rings round me and every time I break into a sprint I feel like I'm going to be sick. I'm blowing out of my arse, booze pouring out of me. When I burp I can taste sambuca. But that wet patch you can see on my chest isn't sweat, it's Vicks. You know the way boozers try to cover up their habit? Well, Vicks was my disguise. If anyone came near me, they couldn't smell the alcohol, but they'd be breathing more easily for weeks. Not that I'm getting anywhere near any of the five Gerrards. They probably haven't even noticed I'm on the pitch.

Liverpool are all over us. Michael Owen is like an out-of-control firework, making tracers all over the pitch. He flashes a shot wide, he hits the bar. Gerrard shakes me off, hits a long, diagonal ball, Owen picks up the pieces and puts

Liverpool in front. I want to be sick. A few minutes later, Nicolas Anelka lays it on a plate for Owen and we're 2-0 down. I ease out another burp.

'How long, ref?'

'Twenty minutes.'

'Fuckin' 'ell ...'

Danny Murphy hits the post, Danny Murphy blazes over, but Anelka makes it 3-0 after Gerrard plays him in.

'Somebody blow the fucking whistle!'

Sat on the coach after the game, I was a man without any self-respect or dignity. That was a sad time, the lowest in my football career. An FA Cup tie against the club I supported as a kid, the club my hero had played for, and I'd embarrassed myself. I didn't even have the decency to turn up in any kind of condition and do myself justice. Instead, I'd spent five days on the piss. What had I become? A bum. A joke. A waster. Staring out of the window on the way back to Birmingham, I thought: 'If you can't even get up for playing at Anfield, it must be over.'

My phone was ringing all the way home but I didn't answer it. They wanted to know what playing at Anfield was like, how good Gerrard was. But I never wanted to talk about it. I knew Gerrard was a better player than me – Alex Ferguson was talking bollocks when he said he wasn't top drawer; he was the best I ever played against by a mile, even if I was half-pissed – but it would have been nice if he'd come away from that game thinking: 'That Curtis Woodhouse is decent.' Instead, he was probably telling his team-mates: 'That Curtis Woodhouse was absolutely shit. Strange really, when he was a kid I thought he'd be good enough to play for Liverpool ...'

CHAPTER 24

KILL OR BE KILLED

I already knew boxers were special. But it took Dale Miles to teach me exactly how special. I hear boxers all the time saying: 'It's going to be a war.' But once you've been in a war, you never want to be in another one. Which is why you often hear boxers promising a war and then, once the first bell goes, they start jabbing and moving. Wars aren't nice. It's you hurting another man and him hurting you. And once you're in one, it can kill you.

It was me who declared war on Dale Miles. At the weigh-in I told him: 'Listen, I'm not running from you.'

'Neither am I.'

'OK, we'll just stand there and duke it out then.'

'No problem.'

And we shook hands.

I lived to tell the tale. And that fight told me I was willing to make the ultimate sacrifice. I'd declared war on a man who had bigger guns than me. In the changing room before-hand, they put these little Everlast gloves on me, with hardly anything in them. They looked like Marigolds. I remember hitting the pads and thinking: 'I'm going to take his head off with these things. This won't go two rounds.' I forgot he was wearing them as well. The first shot he hit me with, I thought: 'Oh. My. God. I'm bang in trouble here.' Too late now – I was over the top and in no-man's land.

When I was growing up in Driffield, there was this big field full of cows with an electric fence around it. Every time he hit me, it took me back to being 10 years old, trying to climb over that fence. This jolt went through my body; I felt like I was being electrocuted. Sat on my stool after round one, I could see my nose under my left eye. A few rounds later, he hit me with a shot and it felt like one side of my face had caved in. Every time he hit me after that, it was as if someone was jabbing it with a red-hot poker. 'What am I doing? Someone get me out of this fight.' That fight was the only time that the thought of quitting went through my head. But I decided to carry on.

In the dressing room afterwards, I said to Ryan Rhodes: 'Why did the bastard referee jump in? He's got to at least give me a chance.'

'Do you know you were down? Curt, you were down heavy in the fifth round. The ref had to stop it, you were fucked.'

I didn't believe him.

At the hospital, they told me my nose was broken and I'd suffered a double fracture of the left cheekbone. That fight was an eliminator for the British title; if I'd won, the dream was in sight. Part of me felt like I'd taken some bullets but dodged the bomb. It made me think something bad was going to happen, somewhere down the line. But, strange as it sounds, I also felt good: 'I've paid my dues, given everything I've got, taken my beating like a man. What more do you want from me?' I always knew I was tough, but it was nice to prove it to other people. If I was willing to go through all that, I was willing to go through anything and still make the correct decision. Which was always to fight on.

What a fight we'd given them. And now it was just me and Charlotte. I was not a pretty picture and she was crying her eyes out. Charlotte tells me that in the back of the ambulance I was talking gibberish, like I was pissed. And now here I was, laid out in a hospital bed, nose bent round the corner, a hole in my face, waiting to be wheeled to the operating theatre. Once the concussion cleared, I started practising my speech in my head. Better get it just right, I thought, for when they all come pouring through the door, to see if I'm alive: 'Don't worry about me – get yourselves off to the party. Did you enjoy the fight? That's the most important thing. I'll be back in the gym in a couple of weeks ...'

I never got to perform it. Not one person came. Not one person rang. I kept checking my phone, thinking: 'Have I got reception in here? Yep, full bars ...' Meanwhile, in a nightclub somewhere, people were probably saying: 'Where's Curtis?'

'I think he's at the hospital.'

'Oh, right. Anyone want a beer?'

That hurt me. The Magna Centre was packed that night.

All my family and friends were there. It was the biggest fight of my career so far and they got their money's worth. But now I was thinking: 'Boxing is just the same as football.' It was an eye-opener. I'd shown the game a lot of love, but it wasn't going to love me back. Once the lights went up, nobody really cared.

Boxing might not love me back but I still hadn't conquered it – as the song says 'I guess I'm just a stubborn kind of fellow' – so I made the correct decision to fight on. Just as important, Dave Coldwell continued to believe in me. I'd left his gym but he was still my manager and we were still in it together. He'd tell me all the time: 'What we're doing is working, we can do this.' He was probably thinking: 'I hope he wins something; I've spent enough money on it.' Before the Dale Miles fight, I joined Dave's promotional company and received a 15-grand signing-on fee. Unfortunately, I had to pay 10 grand to get out of my contract with Frank Warren, so that left me with £5,000. But unlike Frank Warren, everyone at Coldwell Boxing was right behind me, especially Dave and his business partner Spencer Fearn. So three months after getting battered by Dale Miles, Dave rang me and said: 'I've got you a shot at the English title.'

I was thinking: 'I can hardly speak and half my face is caved in.'

What I actually said was: 'Where, when and how much?'

The opponent turned out to be Dave Ryan, a former Midlands Area champion who had lost to Adil Anwar in his own British title eliminator. To be honest, I could have done with easing myself back in, but you don't really get that luxury at domestic level. First time back in the gym I was quite wary, thinking: 'What's gonna happen when I get hit? Is my face gonna fall apart again?' I'd been in a couple of car crashes and it was the same feeling you have when you get behind the wheel again. But I was soon back on it. And I had to be. It didn't matter that I'd become virtually the house fighter at the Magna Centre and people were calling my fight against Dale Miles one of the best they'd ever seen. The losses were stacking up on my record and I wasn't even fighting on Sky, which was now monopolised by Eddie Hearn's Matchroom outfit. One more loss could have proved fatal to my hopes of landing a British title shot.

Not that I was suddenly going to change the way I fought. It's all very well saying that once you've been in a war, you never want to be in another one – I didn't have the necessary cunning to avoid war for too long. Having taken up the game at 26, I didn't have time to learn anything fancy, so I had to try to turn every boxing match into a war to have any chance of winning. That's why I preferred facing people who came to fight, because boxers knew a bit too much for me, were always one step ahead. Plus, the fine art of boxing never really appealed to me; I didn't enjoy watching the sweet science of boxing. My favourite fighters were people like Mike Tyson, Nigel Benn and Arturo Gatti. Like those three, I was never going to be jabbing and moving and trying to sneak through; I was always a wham-bam thank you ma'am, rock 'em and sock 'em, kill or be killed kind of fighter. People used to say to me: 'When I come and see you fight, I know what I'm gonna get.' That gave me a buzz, so I started playing to the crowd a bit, which is always dangerous. But better to go out swinging and getting credit in defeat than fiddling through and losing.

Mum always used to say to me: 'How can you get in the ring, do what you do and then go for a beer afterwards? I thought you hated him?' A friend called Adrian Tolhurst, who sponsored me for one fight, came and watched me spar Jerome Wilson in Rotherham. We went at it hammer and tongs, really let each other have it. Afterwards, Adrian couldn't get his head around it: 'I thought you two were mates?' Most people can't comprehend the idea of deliberately hurting someone they don't even know, let alone know well enough to hate. You've either got the fighting gene or you haven't. But I was always more revved up for a fight when I could stoke up a bit of needle. If an opponent was on Twitter, that was perfect. As soon as the fight was made, I'd get on the phone and start insulting them. I knew they'd take the bait, give me a little bit back and it would help me focus. I used to love that side of the game.

Rarely did I fight somebody I actually disliked. Even when I had a push and a pull with Dave Ryan at our weigh-in, it was because we were tired and hungry, like a couple of old lions who haven't eaten for ages. It's one of the biggest ironies of boxing that those two finely tuned athletes you see on the scales might not have eaten for days. When I first climbed on the scales for the Ryan fight, not a scrap of food had passed my lips for 48 hours. And I was still two pounds over. Dave sent me down to the gym to skip it off in my sweat gear but when I got back, Ryan hadn't turned up yet and I was still one pound over. So off I went to the gym again and this time when I came back I was half a pound under. But there was still no sign of Ryan.

The press were there, waiting to take their photos, and Sky wanted to do an interview but I said to Dave: 'I couldn't give a fuck, I'm not here to do interviews. I'm off.' Not only was I tired and hungry, the adrenaline was pumping through me and sapping my energy. Half of me wanted to lie down and go to sleep, the other half wanted to rip someone's head off. Next thing, Ryan walks in, looking like absolute shit because he's been struggling to make the weight as well. When we do the stare-down, he pushes me in the chest and his manager, Clifton Mitchell, is shouting his head off, telling me Dave Ryan is going to beat the shit out of me. I knew Clifton quite well, because he also did the security at Matchroom shows, but now there were two fighters on the edge and we almost came to blows. Obviously we didn't actually hit each other – we wanted to get paid.

Every time I fought at the Magna Centre it was sprinkled with a little bit of magic dust. Rotherham is a tough, working man's town where the beer is cheap, the women are cheaper and they like their fighting rough and ready. In other words, it was right up my street. Me and Dave Ryan in a ring together was a Rotherham fight fan's wet dream. The fact that it was for the English title and the loser would be staring into a very uncertain future only made it wetter. Our philosophy on boxing was: 'Fuck boxing, let's have a fight.' Neither of us was good enough to get out of the way of the other's punches, so it was a case of: 'You hit me and I'll hit you and whoever falls over first loses.'

At the risk of sounding like some tragic lothario, fighting is like making love to a woman. You become so intimate that a special bond forms, a secret code. You almost become part of each other. And I mean fighting rather than boxing. I just loved fighting, loved that confrontation. Punches flying from all angles, fists whizzing above my head – it was like going over the top in the trenches. Me and Dave Ryan just stood in the middle of the ring and beat each other up. My face was still tender from the Dale Miles fight and, while I'd sparred 20 rounds in camp, that was obviously with a headguard on. So when he hit me, it hurt. And he hit me so hard in the second round I was wobbling all over the place. Everyone must have been thinking: 'Here we go again ...' But I recovered, got through the round and cleared my head. In the third I hit him with one of the best left hooks I ever landed on anyone and he went over. I thought: 'Righto, that's it – game over.' But he somehow got back to his feet and was saved by the bell. For the rest of the fight, we threw the kitchen sink at each other. I got cut in the eighth, could only see out of one eye, but made it to the final bell. And when that final bell sounded, there was this mutual look between us that said: 'You hard bastard.'

Waiting for the scores to be announced, I was thinking: 'Surely I've won. They're not gonna do this to me again?' I wasn't convinced and my heart was coming through my chest. And then I heard those words: 'And the *new* ...'

What a feeling, just this big outpouring of relief. I sank to my knees, before clambering back up again and falling into Dave Coldwell's arms. We'd done it. To come back after that battering by Dale Miles and beat one of the toughest men in British boxing ... I was just so proud of myself. It didn't matter that I was pissing blood for two days. It didn't matter that I couldn't get out of bed. I was champion of England. As for everyone around me, they were no doubt thinking: 'Thank God for that, he's won something. That's your lot.' Because I'd lost a few fights, I could sense that some of the belief around me had started to wane. But I was in balls deep and I wasn't pulling out now. I hadn't promised Dad I'd win the English title. As far as I was concerned, it was either the British title or nothing.

CHAPTER 25

A MAN PISSED

I wish I was one of those people who could blame all my mistakes on others. It must make life easier. But I was too clever for that. I'll never forget coming into training the day before that Liverpool game at Anfield and one of the coaches, Ian Bowyer, catching me brushing my teeth and smothering myself in Vicks. He wasn't an idiot; he knew I'd been boozing. I respected Ian; he was a great player who had won two European Cups with Nottingham Forest. He'd pulled me in loads of times and said: 'Listen, the gaffer really rates you, but you're not helping yourself.' But this time he just gave me a look of disgust. It was horrible. You know when someone wants the best for you, has tried to help and you've let them down? That was the look he gave me and it made me feel even worse. I wish he'd shouted at me. Instead, that look suggested he'd given up on me. I didn't say anything. I just shrugged and sneaked off to training feeling guilty. Out on the training ground, I said to Reg Holdsworth: 'Please mark me, Reg ...' I was bumping into him, tripping over his feet. He knew, too.

Leaving Sheffield United was the worst thing I ever did. I thought every club was like that and I spent the rest of my football career searching for things that didn't exist – the next Russell Slade, the next Steve Myles, the next John Dungworth, the next Mary and Sue. People at Birmingham must have known what had gone on while I was staying at the Hilton – after all, they picked up the tab – but nobody said anything. Maybe Steve Bruce could have dealt with the situation better and tried to help. I'd like to think that if I was a manager and had a young lad who was heading down the wrong path, I'd try to do something. But maybe that's just wishful thinking, me putting a romantic spin on things. Steve Bruce was juggling a lot of stuff – the last thing he needed was some nutter as a distraction. He had to do what was right for the football club, so it made more sense for him to ignore it and focus on the positives. I couldn't blame anyone at Birmingham for my demise. Not Bowyer, not Bruce, not Brady. I might have been a young man but I was also an adult and you've got to help yourself. I wish I could turn back the clock and give myself a good talking to. But I probably would have told my older self to fuck off, get out of my house and never come back. And without darkness, there's no chance of redemption. That's how I have to look at things, to make it easier to live with.

Birmingham finally got promoted that season but I didn't really feel part of the celebrations. My relationship with Bruce disintegrated pretty quickly after his arrival and I soon became a peripheral figure in the squad. I was in the squad that travelled to the playoff final against Norwich in Cardiff but knew I wouldn't be playing. And when we won on penalties, it wasn't really 'we'. I was sat in the dressing room afterwards and there was singing and dancing, corks popping all over the place and champagne being sprayed everywhere. And I was thinking: 'This is horrible. I'd rather be anywhere else but here.'

Instead of getting the team coach back to Birmingham, I jumped in a black cab instead. That night, I went out with Andy Johnson and invited half the people in the nightclub back to my gaff. At some point the next morning, I found someone on my brother's decks in his bedroom. I told him to get out but he didn't listen. So I chinned him. That was my promotion celebration: I took a nightclub, put it in my house and punched someone. What a pickle.

Birmingham, summer 2002

That summer, Bruce brought in a load of new players, including Clinton Morrison from Crystal Palace, Aliou Cisse from Montpellier and Robbie Savage from Leicester. When Sav turned up, I thought: 'Jesus Christ, we've signed Paula Radcliffe.' I just thought he was this bloke with daft hair who could run around all day. But he was actually a lot better than that, good on the ball, a decent passer, very underrated. He was also a sound bloke; I liked him, which might disappoint a few people reading this. But I did see him have the worst fight in football history. There were about six players in the dressing room at the time and a few of us starting winding up Sav and Nico Vaesen over who had the biggest nose. Yeah, I know, not exactly Israel–Palestine. Anyway, Sav and Nico started going at it and there was hairspray, make-up and false nails flying everywhere. Hagler–Hearns it wasn't – more like a couple of girls fighting over a bloke in a nightclub toilet. Tremendous. Sav was very in-your-face in the dressing room but the first time I went out with him in Birmingham, he was like a scared little cat in the corner. It's one thing being loud and brash around other footballers, but in that nightclub around ordinary people he was probably thinking: 'Shit, everyone wants to kill me in here.' Maybe if I'd taken a leaf out of his book, I wouldn't have ended up punching so many people.

With Sav and Cisse added to Bruce's midfield options, the chances of me playing much Premier League football receded. When I was finally sentenced for my part in the curry house punch-up, they virtually disappeared. My solicitor advised me that if I pleaded not guilty and was found guilty, I'd get three years inside, because of my previous record. So I pleaded guilty. I was two hours late for sentencing because I fell asleep in the cab and the driver took me to Nottingham by mistake. But when I finally pitched up, I dodged prison and got 120 hours' community service and a £250 fine. My decision was made easier by the fact that giving evidence were an off-duty police officer and his missus, who'd been on the table next to us, and she claimed it was like a scene from a Wild West movie and was afraid for her life. I laughed in court when she said that, but looking back I realise it must have been scary. I mean, they'd only popped out for a vindaloo and a couple of lagers; next thing they know people are getting smashed over the head with chairs. But I still maintain we didn't start it and came off a lot worse than the restaurant guys did. As I said, that old geezer was very handy.

Because I'd been arguing my innocence for 18 months and suddenly changed my plea to guilty at the last minute, Birmingham obviously weren't best pleased. I'd not been at the club long when it happened, had come with a reputation for trouble, but the club had stood by me. But now that Trevor Francis was gone, there was a new regime in place and a few experienced players had been brought in, I was suddenly expendable. As I've said, in football, you're a commodity. There is no emotional attachment to anyone or anything.

But deep down, there were still embers glowing. I was hurt by what had happened the previous season. We were finally in the Premier League but it had nothing to do with me. So that summer I thought: 'You're signing all these players, you've written me off – I'll fucking show you.' So I did my own pre-season before the actual pre-season. I trained like a maniac for six weeks, didn't touch a drop of alcohol, worked off my belly and tits, got myself in tremendous nick and got the buzz back. But two days before the start of the actual pre-season, someone phoned me up: 'Fancy going out tonight?'

'Nah, pre-season starts on Monday ... where you going?'

'Stoodi Bakers.'

Stoodi Bakers was class.

'I'll come along, but I won't stay long ...'

At 6am on Monday I was absolutely bongoed. I had

training in three hours. I'd gone out on Saturday night and not stopped drinking. On my way to the training ground, I was thinking: 'This is just typical you. You've lived like a monk for six weeks and when you reach the final hurdle, you can't manage it. Instead, you saw that big, shiny red button again and had to press it.' The first thing we did at training that morning was the dreaded bleep test, to assess our fitness. I came last by a country mile.

'Honestly, I've been training like a maniac for six weeks ...'

'Curtis, you obviously haven't ...'

Over the next few days I did enough to get picked for our pre-season tour of Scotland. And now I was thinking: 'Right, I'm inching my way back in here.' But the day before the tour, like a dickhead I went out again, got pissed, booted a post on my way home and jarred my ankle. The next morning it had swollen up like a balloon, so I had to tell Bruce I'd twisted it in training. He took me to Scotland anyway but I couldn't train. The first day of the tour, the lads went out and played golf but obviously I couldn't walk. So Paul Devlin, who didn't like golf anyway, said he'd keep me company. You know what's next. When the lads got back, me and Dev were roaring drunk and Bruce went absolutely mental. He called me a disgrace to the club and every name under the sun. I just told him to fuck off. My plan had been to come back a man possessed. But I actually came back a man pissed. That showed them.

That injury put me out for a fair few weeks and when I finally got back to fitness, Bruce had me training with the kids. He wanted me as far away from the action as possible. I'd get changed in the same dressing room as the first team before having a runaround with the under-15s in a different postcode. I'd stroll into the canteen afterwards and say: 'I was the best player out there by a mile. I'm far too good for that lot – those kids can't handle me.' It was all bravado. Of course I wanted to be training for the big matches against Aston Villa or Liverpool, but I didn't want them to think they were getting to me.

After Bruce had bombed me out, I'd walk into the office on pay day and say: 'Blimey, gaffer, I haven't spent the last lot yet and you're paying me again?!' He'd go bright purple and look like he wanted to kill me. But I couldn't care less. I was just winding him up and knew he couldn't do anything. The club wanted me gone but I still had three years of my contract left to run. I was effectively being paid nine grand a week to loaf about. I was a professional footballer but I wasn't really. I didn't know what I was anymore. Now that I didn't have any commitments, I could do whatever I wanted, even more so than before. There were more doors open than ever, doors that were best left locked.

I started drinking on Fridays and Saturdays as well, so was now drinking seven days a week. I'd finish training, jump in my car, drive home and have the rest of the day to myself, alone with my thoughts and a carrier bag of Stellas. If I'd been playing today, I would have been diagnosed with some kind of illness. A few people suggested I might be suffering with depression. But I didn't ask for help, because I didn't know what depression was or if any help was available. If you had problems, you just got on with it. As an alpha male from Yorkshire, that made perfect sense to me. There were no sports psychologists in my day – just the manager, the coach, the physio and the kit man. I was still only 23, no more than a baby really, rattling around in a big old house. But nobody ever asked me if I was OK; everyone simply assumed I was.

Dad was one of the few people to realise that something was up. He phoned me once and I got all upset: 'I don't know what's going on. I don't want to play, I hate it down here.' Next thing there was a knock on the door. Dad had driven two and a half hours, all the way from Hull, to make sure I was all right. He stayed with me for a couple of days and it must have been very difficult for him to see his eldest son in that kind of state. But when Wayne Quinn came up to visit and told me I didn't seem right, I said to him: 'You should have been out with me last night, I had a great time.' So it's too simplistic to say I was clearly unhappy, because I was still enjoying myself.

But at the same time I felt completely lost, like I was in this dark maze I couldn't escape from. And I did have the odd moment of clarity when I thought: 'How did I get here? This wasn't how things were supposed to pan out.' Somewhere deep inside, I still wanted to be a footballer. Football defined me as a person, whether I liked it or not, and because I'd pressed the self-destruct button and it had been taken away from me, I became disillusioned and down-hearted and upped my drink intake to dilute those feelings. You either wallow in self-pity or you go out and party to make yourself feel better. I chose the latter.

I never graduated to drugs, other than that blissful day

on the beach in Trinidad. But plenty of players were bang on them during my football career, just like young kids in any walk of life. At one club, there was a lad who got done for having weed in his system. It was hushed up but he got a two-week ban. After that, the drugs squad were up at the club all the time. On a Monday morning, we were told: 'Listen, if any of you were messing about at the weekend, doing whatever it is you do, get yourselves home – the drugs lot are here.' You'd end up with about three people training. And every time the drugs squad came in, four of the five lads picked out for testing would be black. I once got tested three times in four days. It was a running joke: 'Random, is it?'

I hated sitting around on Fridays and Saturdays with nothing to do. There was this huge, gaping hole in my life. Because I wasn't even in the squad, I wasn't expected to be at the ground to watch the games. I honestly don't think I was an alcoholic – I was just chasing a high. I lived round the corner from TGI Fridays and I'd sit in there getting smashed all weekend with Tom Williams and Andy Johnson, who were also out of favour. We drank Woo Woos like they were going out of fashion. One afternoon, Karren Brady walked in with a couple of friends. She spotted me at the bar, walked up to me and said: 'I think you should probably leave.'

I dread to think what kind of look I gave her.

'Listen, it's Friday, I've got no game tomorrow and you're not my fucking mum. I'll leave when I want to, thank you very much. Now fuck off and go and sit down.'

I stayed at the bar, drinking as much and as fast as I

could, just to make a point. Obviously I should have left, but I wasn't having her tell me what to do. I hated Karren Brady; I didn't like her at all. I understand that in business you've got to be tough, but I never saw any kind of human side to her. That was the one and only time I spoke to her between the day I signed and the day I left. I played with her husband, Paul Peschisolido, at Sheffield United and he was one of the nicest kids you could ever meet. No idea how he managed to put up with her.

People are probably reading this and thinking: 'I don't get it. You were a professional footballer, what did you have to be down about?' But as a kid, all I thought about was actually playing football. I knew John Barnes was getting paid to play, but I never contemplated that side of the game. I didn't realise that love affairs could be so complicated. I had so much money I couldn't spend it all. But once the football was gone, I was riddled with bitterness and resentment. It was like when you split up with someone and you can't bear the thought of being without them but you absolutely despise them at the same time. Football had given me everything before ripping my insides out and turning me into someone I didn't want to be. You might be living in a five-bedroomed house on a golf course, but if you're sitting on your own, drinking beer, watching shit TV and getting fat, that's no kind of dream.

I didn't want to be drunk the only time I played at Old Trafford. But that's how it was. Whenever there's an article about me in a magazine or on the internet, they often use a picture of me tackling David Beckham. Or trying to. People must think I've got that picture up on the wall, pride of place above the mantelpiece, so that when visitors come round they'll point at it and say: 'Wow! You played against David Beckham at Old Trafford?' But whenever I look at that picture, I feel nothing but disappointment. That picture is a snapshot of how wonderful my life seemed to others but how wrong they actually were. It's a snapshot of me on my footballing deathbed, about to slip into a coma.

I was out on the Thursday, got bongoed as usual, and after training on the Friday we travelled to the hotel in Manchester. Because I felt so rough, and because I was only a substitute, I thought I'd top things up. I remember sitting on the bench, feeling torn: on the one hand wanting to get on; on the other hoping Mathew Sadler, who was only about 17, would make it to the final whistle. Halfway through the second half, he blew a gasket and Bruce sent me on. When I say I was drunk, it wasn't like I was staggering all over the place and slurring my words. But if I'd been tested for drink-driving, there was enough booze in my system to blow the machine up. I was chasing Beckham around like a blue-arsed fly and I could feel it swilling around in my belly. It was so noisy I couldn't hear anything, but I remember think-ing: 'Jesus Christ, I'm playing against Beckham, Keane, Giggs, Veron, Scholes, the whole shebang, and I'm this little fat kid with a hangover.'

Beckham's goal was a peach but it was also my fault: Veron hit a through-ball, I played him onside and he chipped our keeper from about 25 yards. That was just about my last act in my last Premier League game. I can still taste the sambuca just thinking about it.

CHAPTER 26

BUT

Even after I'd won the English title, there were still plenty of 'buts'. I heard that word all the time: 'You boxed well there, but it's only Jimmy Beech . . .'

'You did well against Frankie Gavin, but he obviously didn't train properly . . .'

'You're the English champion, but you'll never win the British title . . .'

'You beat Dave Ryan, but Adil Anwar boxed his head off and you only beat him on a majority decision . . .'

But. But. But. But. But. I was counting buts in my sleep. Most people who had boxed or who wrote about the sport on a regular basis knew I'd already achieved a huge amount. But even my trainer didn't seem too convinced. Glyn Rhodes wasn't the best trainer by any stretch of the imagination. His strength was in the corner on fight night; he was very good at motivating you and saying exactly the right thing at the right time. In fact, he reminded me of Neil Warnock. Against Dave Ryan, after getting cut in the eighth round I sat down on my stool and said: 'I can't see out of my right eye.'

Glyn replied: 'You can't see?'

'No, I can't see anything.'

'All right then . . .'

Glyn started walking towards the referee.

'What the fuck are you doing?!'

'I'm going to stop the fight if you can't see!'

'You can't do that!'

'Well, stop moaning about it, then!'

It was a stroke of genius. Suddenly I was in the room again, utterly refocused: 'All right, I can't see, but I've only got three more rounds to go . . .'

But in Glyn's gym, it was a different story. He ran a lot of boxercise classes that earned him money, so I felt I never got 100 per cent from him. I think Glyn took me on the pads once the whole time I was with him – I wouldn't see him for three or four days at a time. A guy called Les, who was in his sixties, used to take me on the pads or strap on the body bag. I'd smash the granny out of him for 10 rounds, as hard as I could – there were no tactics, no technique. I didn't join the gym for Les to train me; I joined the gym for Glyn Rhodes to train me. He was getting 10 per cent of my money for a job he wasn't doing, which wasn't right.

The final straw came when I got turfed out of the ring because a load of 10-year-old kids were booked in. I only wanted six more minutes but was told to sling my hook. It wasn't as if I thought I was more important than them, but

I was champion of England, the only champion in Glyn's gym. That pissed me off. So a couple of weeks before the first defence of my title, I left. That night in hospital after the Dale Miles fight told me I was right to be utterly selfish in pursuit of this mad dream. I was the one risking life and limb in the ring, so I had to do it my way, even if it meant upsetting a few people along the road.

There had been talk of a rematch with Dave Ryan, but there was no way I was going through all that again for five grand. There were also rumours of me fighting Bristol's Darren Hamilton, who'd only recently beaten Ashley Theophane to land the British title. They wanted it and we wanted it, but we just couldn't make it work and his first defence ended up being against Stevie Williams instead. It was frustrating to be so close and for it not to happen. Instead, my first defence of the English title was against Shayne Singleton.

We were supposed to fight at the Magna in Rotherham, but when I hurt my back it was put back a few weeks and had to be moved to Manchester, Singleton's backyard. I didn't have a choice because I had no money. Every fight was a case of eight weeks' work, earn a few grand, pay off all my debts, repeat the cycle. Even so, the final preparations for the Singleton fight went great and I felt in tiptop shape. Jon Pegg trained me for that fight and he was without a doubt one of the most underrated trainers in Britain. I'd worked with Jon before – he'd offered to help out between rounds when I was sparring Frankie Gavin. Jon gave me a few bits of advice and it made a difference; I did about eight rounds and acquitted myself pretty well. I remember

Frankie saying to me: 'No one causes me problems like you do.' Coming from a former amateur world champion that felt good. So Jon was top of the list when I left Glyn, even though his gym was in Birmingham. If you want the best, sometimes you have to travel to get it.

Manchester, March 2013

I took Shayne Singleton apart, busted him up, shut both his eyes. A lot of my fans didn't stay for the final bell or the decision; they left early because I was so far ahead and Singleton couldn't knock the skin off a rice pudding. It was only when they got home that they found out I'd lost. I couldn't believe it when they announced it was a split decision. I thought I'd won it by miles. So when they gave it to him, this feeling of injustice welled up inside me: 'How can you do this to me? I've put everything into this for seven years and, just like that, you've taken it all away from me and I can't do anything about it.'

It's amazing how tiny, seemingly insignificant things can change the course of somebody's life. Howard Foster, the referee, had taken a point off me with 30 seconds remaining for hitting on the break. I hadn't even been warned and I'd barely touched him; it was a little tap in the ribs. And if he hadn't taken that point off, I wouldn't have lost the fight. He'd blown up the whole plan with a wag of his finger. Before that fight I was ranked fifth or sixth in the country and in line for a British title shot. Suddenly I was back among the also-rans.

The Bowlers Exhibition Centre was an absolute shithole and the crowd that night was like something out of *Shameless*. But even the Mancs were coming up to me afterwards and telling me I'd been robbed. Jamie Moore, who had the same manager as Singleton, had me winning it 8-2. Derry Mathews, who was also ringside, couldn't get his head round it. Dave lost it so badly he was almost hauled in front of the Board of Control. *Boxing News* called it one of the biggest robberies they'd ever seen. Even Singleton knew I'd won it. He couldn't really think anything else – he looked like he'd been in a car crash. But he still behaved like a prick. There's only one thing worse than a bad loser and that's a bad winner – especially if they haven't actually won. If I'd bumped into him afterwards I would have chinned the smug bastard.

I was so angry and upset at being ripped off and cheated. It wasn't just Howard Foster and the judges; it felt like the whole boxing establishment was against me: 'Hang on a minute – I'm putting my all into this game; give me the same chance as you give everyone else.' That inkling I had after my first defeat against Jay Morris, that the boxing blazers didn't want me in their club, had grown into an absolute conviction. By now, I had five losses on my record but it could quite easily have been one. Setanta had me winning the Morris fight by two rounds, Sky had me beating Peter McDonagh by a round, lots of people thought I'd beaten Frankie Gavin, and now pretty much everyone apart from two of the judges thought I'd beaten Shayne Singleton at a canter.

It didn't matter that I actually had a decent jab; the word

was out that I couldn't box so I was never appreciated. Every time it was a close contest, they gave it to the bloke who was actually supposed to be a boxer. I was still an airy-fairy footballer and any success I had in boxing demeaned the sport. I'd broken the mystique: 'What does it say about boxing if this kid can take it up in his mid-twenties and start winning titles? Who does he think he is? Time to put him back in his box.' If I'd come in and got beaten in every fight I'd probably have got more respect: 'What a good lad – isn't he trying hard? Tough, isn't it?' But I'd had the audacity to come in and want to win. I might have been wrong, I might have been paranoid, but that was my mentality. I actually quit for a week; I really meant it. I'd tried to get a rematch with Singleton but they wouldn't give it to me. I was in big trouble: 'Now what do I do? You know what, you finally beat me – stick it up your arse, well done, I'm off. Fuck everyone.'

CHAPTER 27

AWOL

When I met my now wife Charlotte, I was a Premier League footballer. Sort of. Because, as she often likes to point out, I was playing for the reserves. I was in a bar in Solihull with my mate Kelvin, who I'd got to know from training with the youth team, and this girl walked past I liked the look of. I said to Kelvin: 'Fuckin' 'ell, she's all right.' It turned out he went to school with her, so he called her over and we got chatting. That night I had a party back at my house and she came with three or four of her mates, stayed for about five minutes and left. But I phoned her the next day and said: 'I'm in a bar, fancy going for a drink?' She said yes and our first date was in Yates's Wine Lodge. And if anyone knows anything about Yates's, they'll know it's not the sort of wine lodge where you sit around sipping £500 bottles of Château Lafite.

We were stood at the bar and I asked her what she wanted to drink. She said: 'A bottle of white wine.'

'What, to yourself?!'

We ended up having about five bottles between us. And all the time I was thinking: 'This is my kind of girl. As dates go, this is about as good as it gets.' We went out for the next five or six nights in a row. She was only 19 so didn't really know anything about footballers or how they were supposed to look after themselves. But I didn't fall in love with her because of her capacity for drink – although I'll admit it helped – I fell in love with her because she was so different to any girl I'd been with before. When you're a footballer, you can have pretty much any woman you want. But it ends up making you feel vulnerable and insecure, because after the initial novelty has worn off and you're older and wiser, you realise they're only with you for one thing. And that one thing isn't your wit or your dashing good looks. If I'd been a bricklayer, most of the women I went out with wouldn't have come anywhere near me. Footballers are vulnerable and insecure enough, thinking they could be replaced in the team or sold at any moment. Add a load of women into the mix who don't care about you as a person and it adds up to a horrible environment to be in. You wind up in a state of paranoia, always trying to work out people's proper intentions.

But it didn't take me long to work out Charlotte wasn't like that. I wasn't exactly a superstar but even when you're playing for the reserves on a Wednesday every week, some women see you as a golden ticket. Charlotte wasn't all giddy and excited around me like some girls, who are already thinking mansions and Porsches. I had to chase her a little bit and that pissed me off. But it was far better than someone ringing me all the time, asking me to take her to this posh restaurant or that flash bar and talking about some handbag she wanted because some other WAG had one. If you've got anything about you as a man, you see that they're only after one thing. Unfortunately, 99 per cent of women who hang around footballers are like that. There were loads of them in Birmingham; you'd see them in certain bars and they were money-grabbing, attention-seeking, horrible creatures who turned my stomach. But I also blame the footballers, because if you can't see it coming after a while you're a mug who probably deserves to be with one of those cockroaches.

I could relax around Charlotte and I knew straightaway that she was perfect for me. Almost from the off, she was round my house most evenings. We'd have something to eat, watch a film and she'd go home because she had to be up for work the following morning. I knew she liked me for the right reasons, none of which was money. She wasn't even interested in the fact that I played football. Her dad is a Birmingham City season ticket holder so her family knew who I was. But she never once saw me play. If you were to ask her what teams I played for, she wouldn't have a clue after Sheffield United and Birmingham. And that's just how I like it. I couldn't be doing with someone pretending they know what they're talking about and getting involved in my job. She was a good'un and I was going to keep hold of her. Me and Sunderland, or me and Glasgow Rangers might have been a pretty good fit. But I wouldn't have met Charlotte, which cancels out any regrets. I always say to young players now: 'When you find a good'un, do not let go of her, because there aren't many of them about.'

When I speak to my old team-mates now, most of them have split up with the missus they met when they were playing and earning a fair few quid. Suddenly, they weren't quite as alluring when they were running a pub. When Charlotte met me I was living in a massive house and driving a dirty great Lexus jeep. But that was the moment it all went to shit. I sometimes say to her: 'I was like the *Titanic* and you were the iceberg!' Then again, I'm not big on blondes, so she should probably count herself lucky . . .

Not long after that game at Old Trafford, Steve Bruce pulled me into his office and said: 'Blackpool have come in for you – they want to take you on loan.'

'Listen, gaffer, let's just get a few things straight: the only time I ever go to Blackpool is on stag dos. Don't call me into your office unless someone in Yorkshire comes in for me. Otherwise, I ain't going nowhere.'

Steve Coppell was interested in taking me to Brighton, and Grimsby also fancied me. Then Bruce called me into his office again and told me Rotherham were sniffing around but couldn't afford my wages. At first I refused to go. But then those embers started glowing again. Birmingham were desperate to get me out of the door and deep down I still wanted to play football. So suddenly Charlotte wasn't going out with a Premier League footballer; she was going out with someone who played for Rotherham in the First Division. And I'll give you a clue – they weren't paying me nine grand a week. All aboard the lifeboat . . .

I had a decent run at Rotherham, actually played pretty well. We blew up down the home straight and missed out on the playoffs but it was a good little club. I was back in York-shire and it was nice to be around a few of my old mates. Unluckily for Bruce, the loan deal was only for three months so I was back at Birmingham before the end of the season. But not for long. One day after pre-season training, I said to my brother: 'Fancy going on holiday?'

'What do you mean? What about training?'

'Bollocks to training.'

'Where do you wanna go?'

'Anywhere. I'm not bothered.'

'I'll pack my suitcase . . .'

We went to Marbella. We went to Tenerife. We went to Scotland. We went to so many places that when they finally tracked me down, I couldn't tell them where I'd been. Steve Bruce did phone me, to try to get me to come home: 'Curtis, when are you coming back?'

'Whenever . . .'

Before the FA hearing, my solicitor told me I'd been AWOL for 44 days. I remember thinking: 'Fuckin' 'ell, 44 days. Good effort.' I don't recall much about the hearing itself. I do remember I was wearing a pair of grey tracksuit bottoms with Guinness all down them. I do remember I hadn't shaved for about a month, was sweating like a lunatic and stank of tequila. So it was me, my solicitor and Gordon Taylor, the head of the Professional Footballers' Association, sat opposite Steve Bruce, Karren Brady and David Sullivan. I don't recollect swearing my head off; I was only told that later. But I do remember thinking: 'I don't care what they do – just get me out of this room. I want a Diet Coke, I think I might pass out . . .'

I still had two years left on my contract and was owed about £2.5m in wages. But I just didn't care. I thought everyone was out to get me. I thought nobody wanted to help. I thought Steve Bruce was a wanker. I thought Karren Brady was a bitch. When I was smashing up Indian restaurants and playing for the first team, they pretended it didn't happen. But now I was a mess, they wanted me off the wage bill. I couldn't tell you what was said or even the official reason I got sacked. I haven't got a clue, because I wasn't really there.

CHAPTER 28

TROLL HUNTER

I hear them when I'm sat ringside, these dickheads with eight or nine pints inside them, telling fighters they're useless. I feel like turning round and chinning them. They've got no respect. Here are two men putting their lives at risk for their entertainment and these idiots are calling them 'bums'. As an ex-boxer, I can tell by looking at a fighter what he's going through. But you hear these drunken idiots, watching with their pissed mates, saying things like: 'Why has he not got up there?!' Because he doesn't know what day it is. 'He should have taken a knee! Why has he got up so quick?!' Because he thinks it's next week. Whenever I went down, it was because I had my lights switched off. I never voluntarily went down and thought: 'Oh, perhaps I should take a knee, just to clear my head. After all, that pissed bloke called Steve in the crowd has just said I should.

Thanks, Steve! I'd never have it done it without you! You prick . . .'

The keyboard warriors, those wankers crouched over their laptops at 3am with a box of Kleenex and this raging hatred of themselves, are even worse. I was used to criticism from my football career – half the people in the pub thought they were better than me – but I got out before social media kicked in. After I'd started boxing and gone on Twitter, some of the abuse was disgusting. I'd dedicated my life to this sport, pumped every penny I'd earned from football into this dream, so I thought I deserved some respect. And, for the most part, that's what I got. But there were also quite a lot of people prodding me with a stick, taking the piss and laughing at me. 'Failed boxer, failed footballer' – that was a common one. You can dress it up however you like, but it comes down to pure, unadulterated jealousy. Success hurts a lot of people and someone trying to succeed hurts a lot of people even more. It means they have to evaluate their own lives and ask themselves why they're not successful or trying to be successful themselves. These are people who probably dreamed of being footballers or boxers as kids but didn't come close. And they think the only reason I boxed or played football was because I was talented. Bollocks. Truth is, I worked so hard to make it as a professional footballer and was working even harder to make something of myself in boxing. They knew that deep down and it hurt them. So they made themselves feel better by spewing bile.

One particular troll chose the wrong moment to crawl out of his hole. He'd started messaging me six months earlier, after I'd tweeted something really mundane about finishing the school run and driving to training. He tweeted me back: 'You want to be careful when you take the kids to school – you never know who's watching.' That got the alarm bells ringing, so I sent one back: 'I'm all for a bit of banter but you want to be careful what you say to people, because you never know who's going to turn up on your doorstep, either.' He kept this up periodically and a couple of weeks before the Singleton fight, he sent a tweet calling Charlotte a 'fucking bitch'. Because it was so close to the fight, I decided to let it slide. But after the fight, he chirped up again. Bear in mind I've just been robbed, my career's in tatters, I hate the world, I am very, very angry and upset. And now this wanker is taking the piss:

@jimmyob88 @woodhousecurtis retire immediately cant even defend a pathetic little title you are a complete disgrace #awfulboxer

@jimmyob88 @woodhousecurtis Whats funny u put so much effort in sacrificed all that time and failed to defend your mickey mouse title #wasteofspunk

They were the straws that broke the camel's back. I decided to put a bounty on his head:

@woodhousecurtis @jimmyob88 i'll give £1000 to anybody that provides me with address and picture of this man! knock knock!!

@jimmyob88 @woodhousecurtis what u going to do
knock me out like your last opponent ooops

Suddenly, everyone is retweeting my tweet and it's
almost breaking the internet. Within minutes, a mate from
Sheffield called me and said he knew who it was. As luck
would have it, my mate was an estate agent and had sold
this bloke his house a few weeks earlier, so he emailed me
over the whole shebang: the street he lived on (he wouldn't
tell me the number – he didn't want to be an accessory to
murder), how much he paid for his house, even the name
of the football team he played for and their fixture list, so
I knew where he was going to be every Sunday. I was one
step ahead of him, the only thing I didn't have was his diary.

@woodhousecurtis @jimmyob88 james o brian, mount
view road, you silly silly boy, see you really soon big
boy

Now, it's going absolutely mental on Twitter. Meanwhile,
I've jumped in the car and hit the road.

@woodhousecurtis @jimmyob88 old jimmy has shit
his pants and gone quiet because we know where he
lives! we are coming over for a brew

@jimmyob88 @woodhousecurtis chill out pal i was
only doing it so you would bite back it was only a bit
of harmless fun

@woodhousecurtis just on my way to sheffield to have a little chat with an old friend, get the kettle on @jimmyob88 #boxing #football #sillysillyboy

@woodhousecurtis can somebody let me know what number it is?? i know it's mount view road just need the number, i'll send a pic when i arrive

@woodhousecurtis he's gone very quiet!

@jimmyob88 @woodhousecurtis i was only joking about Didnt think you would be bothered thought you would take them as a joke

@woodhousecurtis too late for that now jimmy, i've had enough of your mouth, i'll be about 50 minutes and you can have your say then

@woodhousecurtis sat nav says i'm 47 minutes away, i'm getting a hard on!! @jimmyob88

By now, it feels like the whole country is cheering me on, as if I'm some sort of superhero on a mission to rid the world of Twitter trolls:

@Ben_9 @woodhousecurtis aka Liam Neeson!! Haha how on earth you managed to track him down is beyond me. #MakeHimPay

When I arrived, I took a photo of his road sign and
tweeted it:

@woodhousecurtis right Jimbob i'm here !!!!! someone
tell me what number he lives at, or do I have to knock
on every door #it's showtime

Now I've got the likes of Lennox Lewis, Joey Barton and
John Prescott tweeting about it, as well as what seems like
everyone else in the country:

@LennoxLewis Ha! I LOVE this story about
@woodhousecurtis paying a visit to a #keyboard
warrior on Twitter

@Joey7Barton I'm not an advocate of violence but
what @woodhousecurtis has just done is hilarious.
Another big mouth left with sh*tty undies

@johnprescott THIS is how we deal with things in
Hull. Boxer @woodhousecurtis tracks down a Twitter
troll to his street!

@ChrisMcf1982 shows what happens when boys with
destructive fingers anger men with destructive fists!!
#knockknock

Now this kid is shitting himself:

@jimmyob88 @woodhousecurtis i am sorry its getting
a bit out of hand i am in the wrong i accept that

By the time I got there I'd calmed down and was finding
the whole thing funny, which was just as well because if I
had done anything there would have been about five million
witnesses. But I didn't want to let him off that easily. I had
a sponsored car at the time with my name emblazoned all
over it, so I was circling this cul-de-sac like a shark, tweeting
and watching to see if there were any curtains twitching. But
after half an hour, I decided to call off the hunt:

@woodhousecurtis never came out to play so i'm going
back home! maybe a bit daft what i did today but
sometimes enough is enough

It might have seemed a bit daft to some – as quite a few
people pointed out, why didn't I just block him?! – but I
never take the easy option. I wasn't thinking about blocking
him; I wanted to kill him! What you've got to remember is, I
didn't know this James O'Brien. He might have been 6ft 7in
tall and a complete nutcase. He might actually have been
hanging around my kids' school. So I was thinking: 'What if
I go home one day, something's happened to my family and
I didn't do anything about it?' I'd have to live with that for
the rest of my life. So no wonder I decided: 'I'll put an end
to this now.'

My anxiety, which I've had since those dark days in
Northfield Crescent, played a big part in it. Since then,
I've never been able to sleep properly, three or four hours

is a good night for me. Sometimes even now I sleep on the settee downstairs, because I've convinced myself something bad is going to happen and it's all going to go crazy. I get that same tight chest I had when I was a kid, waiting for Mum and Dad to come crashing through the door. A coin spinning in my head. It's difficult to explain anxiety to people without sounding like a loon. Long before Jimmy Brownpants came on the scene, I'd be half a mile into a seven-mile run, see a car go past and convince myself it was heading to my house to kidnap Charlotte and the kids. I'd picture it in my head as I was running and eventually have to turn around and sprint back. Charlotte would say: 'Why are you back so early?' And I'd have to tell her I was only doing a short run that day. But the fact that nothing has actually happened doesn't make it any better; it simply means the anxiety is never-ending. You're always building up to this explosion that never goes off, so you're fucked both ways.

I'm also a bit obsessed with death, probably because of Dad and Uncle Carson passing away. Death panics me all the time: 'What if someone knocks on the door and tells me Mum is dead? What if that car suddenly veers right and kills us all?' At the same time, I don't really want to get old because the older you get, the more you see people around you dying. It sounds selfish, but I'd rather be the first to go.

The morning after the day before and I'd got myself 9,000 new Twitter followers. Newspapers in America, Australia and Canada were writing about it and people were tweeting me addresses of trolls they wanted sorting out. A mate told me all the lads were slaughtering Jimmy Brownpants in the local boozer: 'You shit your pants! Wanker!' Then I got a call from the people at *Daybreak*, asking if I wanted to go on the show and discuss it with Lorraine Kelly.

So I'm in this room, getting my make-up done, and Lorraine walks in: 'Just to let you know, we've also got James on the show.'

This was the first time they'd told me.

'Oh, right.'

'And this isn't *Jeremy Kyle*. We don't have any security.'

'Right.'

'Are you going to attack him?'

'If I go on and he starts talking shit, I can 100 per cent guarantee he's gonna get walloped.'

So Lorraine scurries off and comes back five minutes later.

'We've just spoken to James and all he wants to do is apologise. He's really scared. He doesn't want to come out if you're going to attack him . . .'

I hate admitting this, but when I was sat on the sofa and saw him walk out, I felt sorry for him. He looked so vulnerable. I'd have preferred it if he was 6ft 7in tall and looked like a complete nutcase. Instead, he was this skinny little kid shuffling on and I suddenly felt like I was the bully. I had to remind myself that this fella had been taking liberties, and not just with me. He'd also been abusing Lennox Lewis, Victoria Beckham, Rio Ferdinand and Katie Price's disabled son. That was clearly the highlight of his day, sending people horrible messages. Unfortunately for him, while Lennox Lewis lives in America, I live 45 minutes down the road. Anyway, he apologised, we shook hands and I had a nice new nickname. People often say to me: 'Oh, you're that Troll Hunter?' I'll be thinking: 'Fuck me, I played over 400 games of professional football, won titles in professional boxing and there are loads of people out there who only know me as that bloke who chased some dickhead off the internet.'

Quite funny, actually. And hunting trolls certainly puts a spring in your step.

CHAPTER 29

SLOWLY BURNING

Birmingham, autumn 2003

So, this is how the dream turned out: sat in my pants drinking Stella, trying to blot out the memories of a failed career. Football had consumed me for so long and I ended up hating it. But, as with any long-term relationship, however dysfunctional, parting wasn't easy. I was just so upset and had absolutely no self-respect: 'How have you managed to become a fat drunk when you have all this talent?'

Part of me wished my football career had never happened, just like you wish you'd never met that woman you ended up hating. There was no pride in my achievements – I saw everything as one big waste. My football career was the equivalent of Ricky Hatton winning the British title and nothing else. If Ricky Hatton had only won the British title, he wouldn't wake up every morning thinking: 'Wow, I did great.' He'd wake up thinking: 'Jesus, what a fuck-up. I should have been a world champion.' I was a very good footballer and I massively underachieved. I should have played in the Premier League for most of my career. Even my international caps meant nothing, because I should have played for the full England team in major tournaments. So almost as soon as I was done at Birmingham, I tried to erase it all from my memory.

People would ask me: 'Do you remember that game and do you remember that goal? What was it like to play against Beckham at Old Trafford? How good was Steven Gerrard? How great did it feel to be playing for your country?' And I genuinely wouldn't be able to remember some of it, because you tend only to hold on to the good stuff. For years I didn't watch football or want anyone talking about football around me, because it made the disappointment and anger bubble up inside me. It would have been a lot easier to live with if I'd been badly injured. It was nobody else's fault. All the blame was on me, so my football career was an embarrassing episode I wanted to bury for good.

I could sense their excitement but I couldn't share it. 'Can we talk about something else? Did you see *East-Enders* the other day?' A lot of people probably walked away thinking: 'What a miserable prick.' But they wouldn't keep asking you about your ex-wife after a divorce. And you wouldn't keep any photos of her either. There wasn't – and still isn't – one photograph of me playing football in my house. I chucked out all my newspaper clippings and all my shirts, even the England ones. The player of the year trophy I won at Sheffield United is gone as well. They were all reminders of my potential and how much I'd pissed away. People would give their right arm for my football career on paper – over 300 league games, England caps, playing in the Premier League – but, to me, it was just a mountain of regret, shame and frustration.

With the benefit of hindsight, I realise that my football career was never destined to be a long-drawn-out affair. I get bored very easily and need to be constantly stimulated. That's why I have very few friends I speak to regularly, because I can be difficult to be around for long periods. As soon as I finish a meal in a restaurant, I want out of there. I'm there to do a job, which is to fill my belly. Once I've done that, it's mission accomplished; I don't want to sit around chatting. Tick the box, let's go and do something else. Problem was, once I'd been binned by Birmingham, I didn't have anything else to do, other than wallow in bitterness. The sacking was the crash; now I was slowly burning.

When I say I didn't have anything else to do, I'm not being entirely honest. Because three months after we met, Charlotte fell pregnant. That was a massive shock, for both of us. I was only 23; Charlotte had only just turned 20. One minute we were necking bottles of wine in Yates's Wine Lodge, the next we were supposed to be adults. I'd never even thought about having kids, so my first reaction was: 'Oh, fuck.' That initial shock eventually gave way to excitement. I remember them putting something on Charlotte's belly at the first scan and the baby's heart hammering away at 100mph. That was an amazing moment, made it feel real. When Kyle first came out, he wasn't breathing. It felt like forever but it was only 10 seconds. I thought he was dead but one of the nurses blew in his face and he started screaming his head off. What a moment – almost impossible to top. Almost . . .

I went back to my house, broke out the beers and got absolutely bollocksed with Dad and my brother. But at six in the morning, I suddenly decided I wanted to see my baby again. So I jumped in the car and drove to the hospital. When I finally got there, I started banging on the door and shouting: 'I'm with Charlotte! I wanna see my son!' Charlotte could hear me and was mortified. I was effing and blinding but the nurse insisted I wasn't allowed in until 10 o'clock. I tried to kip on a bench but it was bloody freezing, so I got back in my car, cranked the heating up and fell into a deep sleep. When I woke up it was bright sunshine and the car park was full, but the batteries had gone on my car and my phone so I didn't know what time it was. I ran up to the maternity ward and discovered it was one in the afternoon. Everyone had been there since 10, so when I staggered in, still steaming and looking like I'd been dragged through a hedge, there was this big: 'Congratulations!' But not from Charlotte; she just looked at me in utter disgust.

Charlotte had only known me a year so didn't really have an idea of what kind of dad I'd be. In those early weeks, it wasn't a good one. It was a few months later that I went AWOL for 44 days, leaving Charlotte to look after the baby on her own. She thought it was the responsibility of having

Kyle that sent me off the rails, but that was only part of it. I hadn't told her I'd fallen out of love with football and it was drowning me. I was in need of a guardian angel, someone to dive in and drag me out. And then one day the phone went: 'Curtis? Barry Fry. You wanna come and play for me at Peterborough?' Proof that angels come in all shapes and sizes.

CHAPTER 30

A WHIMPER

I announced my retirement on Twitter; told anyone who wanted to know that the sport had ripped my heart out. Charlotte had wanted me to retire after my first fight against the Mexican Window Cleaner. It was tough for her to watch me kill myself in training, get battered in the ring and pick up the pieces afterwards. The weekend she spent with me in hospital after the Dale Miles fight, we were supposed to be celebrating her 30th birthday. Instead, she tended to my injuries. Other times, she had to help me off the settee and out of the bath.

All the punishment I'd taken was catching up with me. If you're a game, come-forward fighter like me, you get hit an awful lot. Suddenly the punches started hurting a lot more – shots that used to bounce off me were making me wince. I started getting headaches and forgetting things. I'd say to Charlotte: 'Have I always been like this?' And she'd have to admit I hadn't. I'd only had 22 fights by this stage, but people forget that boxers don't just take punishment on fight night; they take plenty more in sparring, especially if, like me, they're not very good. I sparred Ryan Rhodes before his fight against Saul Alvarez in 2011 and he put me in hospital with concussion. I was sat on the edge of the ring after the session and he said to me: 'You sparred well there, Curt.' All of a sudden I could see the walls coming towards me and it was getting darker and darker. Eventually, the whole room went black.

Having the kids find out I'd lost wasn't nice either. After a fight, as soon as I was back in the dressing room, I'd phone them up to tell them how I'd got on. If I'd lost, that was a horrible call to have to make. I'd walk through the front door, my face would be a mess and they must have been looking at me, thinking: 'Blimey, is this what normal dads do?' I wanted to be their superhero, like my dad was my superhero. Instead, I just felt dehumanised. Like a bum.

We'd massively downsized but the family had grown to five – Caleb had arrived in 2012 – and the five-bedroomed house in Hull had been replaced by a little house in Newport, a village in the East Riding of Yorkshire. The boxing really put us in the shit financially. Bills weren't being paid and we were way behind with the mortgage. Throughout my football career, I never lent anyone in my family money; they were all too proud to ask. But now I was tapping up Mum for a few quid here and there, just to get me through training camps.

Meanwhile, Charlotte was miles from her family and

friends in Birmingham, holding the fort while I was off pursuing a dream that she probably didn't even care about. I'm not sure I would have been prepared to follow her dream for all that time. One day she was going out with a Premier League footballer (or kind of), the next she was living in a little house in the middle of nowhere, looking after three kids and making me dinner every night because I was too knackered to get out of my chair. Living with a boxer must be seriously weird. I'd have to watch the kids eating fish and chips while I was tucking into some broccoli, having just done a seven-mile run. Charlotte used to hide the crisps and sweets in the washing machine and hear me creeping around at three in the morning, hunting for chocolate. It must have been like living with a smackhead.

I'm very much like Dad; I don't sit down with my wife and talk about my feelings: 'You have your say, I'll have my say, let's have a cuddle.' She never questioned anything. If she had, I would have told her to suck it up. But that conversation never had to happen. She followed me from pillar to post during my football career (she fell pregnant with Isla in Peterborough, gave birth to her in Grimsby and in between we lived in Hull), and she'd also been at every fight but one. She'd taken time out of every single day to make sure dinner was prepared when I came home from training. She'd taken sole care of my children while I was in camp. That means so much more than all that lovey-dovey bullshit. Most women would have left me years earlier, especially the type who set out to snag a footballer as a husband. But it was love that kept her there. I knew 100 per cent she loved me because she proved it in so many ways. Charlotte has seen the bad, the ugly and not much good. I'm not gushy, but she means the world to me.

Ironically, her loyalty played a big part in me reversing my decision to retire. Just knowing that she would support anything I decided to do was key. I was also inundated with messages from people in boxing I respected, telling me to plough on. And what else was I going to do? Sit about watching *Emmerdale*? That wasn't going to achieve anything. I didn't want to be remembered as that bloke who messed up two things in life, so it was important to keep plugging away just so I could sleep at night. And if you thought too much about what other people thought, even your own kids, you'd rot away. Daddy had to do what Daddy had to do. And I had a promise to keep to my own superhero.

If everyone I fought was as bad as Sandor Horvath, I'd have carried on until I was 80. How he had nine wins on his record and where they found him I do not know, but he was the worst kid ever to put on a pair of gloves. It looked like they'd dragged him off the street – everything about him was just wrong. In other words, he was absolutely perfect for me after the run of fights I'd just had. I put him away in just over a minute, but I can't believe it took me that long. That fight was my first at lightweight and dropping down was a bit of a gamble to say the least. Not only did it mean losing a few extra pounds, but the lightweight division was stacked with talent, with Derry Mathews, Kevin Mitchell, Gavin Rees and Tommy Coyle standing between me and a shot at the British title. Tommy is from Hull, so I'd been baiting him on Twitter and Facebook for months, trying to lure him up to light-welterweight. At one point it looked like it might happen down at lightweight, and that would have been the biggest fight in that part of Yorkshire for years, but the stars never aligned.

But another boxer from Hull did play a huge part in my career, even though we never actually met in the ring. Luke Campbell won gold at the London Olympics and Eddie Hearn was on a mission to make him the first boxer from the city to win a major title. When Campbell fought in Hull it meant opportunities for local fighters to appear on the same bill, and fighting on the same bill as Campbell meant television exposure. So in the summer of 2013, I found myself walking out at Craven Park at 5pm, with the sun shining and the smell of sizzling burgers in my nostrils. I didn't really feel like having a fight; I felt like having a glass of wine and a nap in a deckchair. Fighting when it was light didn't feel right; for some reason it was quite unnerving. Hull KR's ground seats 12,000, but I was first on and there must have been about 500 people in the crowd. Most people were only interested in seeing Campbell make his debut. I felt like one of those singers performing to no one in a forgotten corner of a festival.

Despite those misgivings, I put in one of my best performances against Joe Elfidh. I'd had a really good training camp with Jon Pegg, who'd taught me how to cut the ring off more effectively. And once I'd cornered Elfidh, I was punch-perfect, dropping him three times before stopping him in the third. On the same bill, Tommy Coyle was stopped by Derry Mathews in a match for the Commonwealth lightweight title, which put paid to any idea of an

East Riding Extravaganza. There was some talk about me fighting Kevin Mitchell, but Dave said to me: 'If you want my advice, stay well away from Kevin Mitchell. It's not a fight you really need.' That's boxing code for: 'He'll fucking kill you.' But Dave also managed Derry, so me against him was a natural fight. Though there was nothing natural about my preparations.

I'd sparred Derry in preparation for the Singleton fight so knew he was a good fighter. He'd had 40-odd pro fights, 100-odd amateur fights, and had a reputation as being a really tough kid. I was under no illusion that he was a big step up in class. But I was beginning to get desperate. I'd just lost my English title, had tumbled down the light-welterweight rankings, and thought that if I beat Derry I'd finally get a crack at a British title. Everyone had advised me not to drop down. I remember Jamie Moore, the former British light-middleweight champion, saying to me: 'What on earth are you doing moving down to lightweight – you're a big light-welter!' The truth is, I would have moved down to flyweight if it'd meant getting a shot at the British title. I never thought about my health. And anyway, I figured losing a few extra pounds would mean I'd need to be even more disciplined than usual. I'd fought up at light-middleweight before and was nowhere near as fit as when I was down at light-welter. Plus, the two fights I'd had at lightweight lulled me into a false sense of security, because I'd walked through both opponents and barely taken a punch. Plus, how could a lightweight do me any damage when neither Ryan Rhodes nor Kell Brook had ever put me down in sparring?

I did most of my training at about 10st 7lb and looked

really sharp. When I started tapering down, about 10 days before the fight, I was on fire. People around me were probably thinking I was going to take Derry Mathews apart. But crashing from 10st 7lb to 9st 9lb tears your body apart. Your speed goes, your hand-eye co-ordination goes, your reflexes go, your punch resistance goes. From being on fire, suddenly I was all burnt out. A week before the fight, a doctor measured my hydration and body fat levels. I was nine and a half pounds over the lightweight limit but my body fat was 4.6 per cent. Anything below 5 per cent and you're in the danger zone. I didn't dare tell the doctor what weight I was fighting at. The last few days before the fight I was drinking four litres of water a day and eating nothing. I'd get out of bed and go for a run on no fuel whatsoever.

At the press conference two days before the fight, my ears started popping and it felt as if they were bleeding. While we were sat up on the dais, Derry leaned forward, turned to me and said with a big smile: 'You're fucked, mate.' He knew because he'd been through it himself: when he fought Martin Lindsay a few years earlier, he went from light-welterweight to featherweight in a couple of months. I just smiled back at him. There were a few more barbs slung in both directions but my heart wasn't in it. My eyes were glazed, my skin was like a film pulled tight across my skull and I couldn't really hear him anyway. I just wanted to get back to my hotel and have a lie down.

When I got back to my room, I was 10st 4lb, nine pounds over the lightweight limit. I went for a run and lost two more pounds, but when I woke up the following morning I was still six pounds over. So it was back out for a run before climbing in the sauna to boil myself down to nothing. I made weight but even as I flexed my muscles on the scales, I knew I was in serious trouble. I ordered a Nando's after the weigh-in but eating was difficult because my stomach had shrivelled up so much. So I left most of it, drank and drank and drank and went to bed. I felt like I could have slept for days. Unfortunately, I had to fight one of the hardest boxers in Britain the following evening, in front of a couple of thousand screaming Scousers at the Liverpool Olympia.

In the dressing room before the fight, I was all over the place. I was missing the pads and, when I was called to the ring, I tripped over a wire on my way out. Leading up to fights, I always had the feeling something bad was going to happen, because of all the stress and pressure I was under. But that was the only time I ever walked to a ring knowing I was going to lose. It was a horrible feeling. And not only did I know I was going to lose, I thought I might get very badly injured. Or worse. I climbed into the ring that night weighing 11st 4lb, which meant I'd put on 25lb in about 34 hours. All that does is tell you how dangerously dehydrated I was in the first place, and a lot of the fluid I'd lost around the brain wouldn't have been replaced. I just wanted to get home safely to my family. But Derry couldn't care less about any of that.

Despite all my fears, my game plan was to stay close and turn it into a dogfight. Same as it ever was. But if the fight had gone long, that could have been my career over. Or worse. Luckily, it didn't. In the fourth, he clipped me with a right hand and I went over. When I got back to my feet, I was staggering all over the place and the referee stopped it.

That was a tough pill to swallow because I never got into the fight. I wanted to box on after the knockdown but my body wouldn't let me. On the flipside, if I had done I might have ended up in a wooden box.

You'd think that fight – for the Commonwealth title and live on Sky – would at least have earned me some decent money. But I only got eight grand. Once I'd paid my normal connections, my travel costs between Yorkshire and Birmingham and a nutritionist I'd hired specially for that fight, I came out with about £4,000. And for what? That was the daftest fight I ever took. I thought I could have beaten Derry at 10st, but at 9st 9lb I couldn't beat his granny.

That whole period down at lightweight was attempted career suicide. Once you take that kind of weight off for a sustained period, you're never really the same again, especially if you're getting on a bit. But the emotional damage was even worse. Before when I'd lost I'd gone down swinging, but this time I'd gone out with a whimper. That hurt my pride. And I felt like I had nowhere left to go. I'd lost my belt and ranking at light-welterweight, and moved down to lightweight; I'd had to twist people's arms to get me a shot at the Commonwealth title and then not put up a fight. Now what? It's not as if I could have gone down to super-feather. I shut myself away and was consumed by darkness, groping about for lifelines that didn't exist. I felt like I was suffocating. The reality was beginning to close in on me: 'I'm not gonna do this.'

CHAPTER 31

THE STARS ALIGN

If I'd been in my right mind I would have walked away after being knocked out by Derry Mathews. But I wasn't really in my right mind. The worst thing I did was promise Dad I'd win the British title. If I could have turned back time, I would never have made that promise. It really ate away at me and was very difficult to handle, especially after losses. I spent many sleepless nights wondering what would happen if I didn't keep that promise. And I was constantly haunted by the conclusions. I would have had to accept that I was wrong, almost everyone else was right and a whole chunk of my life had been a lie. And I have no doubt it would have sent my life, and the lives of those around me, spiralling out of control.

There is a strange symmetry between my football and boxing careers. There were lots of occasions when I could have turned my football career around simply by sacrificing a few weeks of my life, but I could never take that last step. Like the time I got myself fit before pre-season at Birmingham before booting a post and busting my ankle. But just as I could have turned my football career around on lots of occasions, I could have quit boxing hundreds of times but didn't. It's all part of my psychological make-up. I found football easy, so subconsciously I was probably thinking: 'I've already made it – why do I need to keep making it again and again?' But I still hadn't conquered boxing. I was still in the foothills.

When I first told people I was going to be a British champion, they said: 'No, Curtis, you won't be. You're getting beaten up in sparring by people who are shit.' They'd give me this look that said: 'What a knobhead.' A year later, I was beating those same kids up. But unlike with football, I was always winging it a little bit in boxing. I still really thought it would happen, but most people didn't believe I could achieve this great thing. Some were still laughing at me, especially after my loss to Derry Mathews. But that was yet another assault on my ego. If you challenge me and tell me I can't do something, I'll go out and prove you wrong. Whenever it looked like there was no way back, I'd think: 'I can't end it like this, I can't fuck it all up again, I can't let Dad down – I'll just have to find one. Fuck you. Fuck everyone.'

But there's no getting away from the fact that they were dark, scary times. I knew I wouldn't have to get to 40-0 to land a shot at a British title, but the losses were mounting up and I was sliding down the rankings. Not only did a British title challenge seem further away than ever, but I was past my best, disintegrating physically. Sparring was becoming more and more difficult. As well as the headaches, my knees were knackered, which made roadwork difficult, which in turn made making weight even more of a nightmare. But Dave was still on board, constantly telling me: 'I'll do anything I can to get you that fight.' By now, I would have taken the fight for nothing. I needed it that badly.

After the Mathews defeat I stopped working with Jon Pegg. Jon had taught me so much and if I'd lived in Birmingham I would have spent the rest of my career with him. But the travelling and being away from home were killing me. So I gave Ryan Rhodes a call and asked if he'd train me for my next fight. Ryan was doing some keep-fit training at the time and was reluctant at first: 'You do know I'm not a boxing trainer?' But he was someone I'd looked up to for years, who'd had more than 50 pro fights and knew more about the game than almost anyone.

My comeback fight was against Lewis van Poetsch on another Luke Campbell card in Hull, only six weeks after losing to Mathews. Van Poetsch, a serving soldier who had won only three of seven pro fights, was meant to be an easy touch, all about getting back on the ladder before hanging on for favours and a bit of luck – maybe the football angle hadn't quite worn off yet and a promoter would see the benefit? But that night just about summed up my boxing career. I was absolutely ripped, despite being two divisions heavier than I was for the Mathews fight, which shows you how drained I'd been down at lightweight. But Van Poetsch turned out to be as tough as his army boots – if all of our soldiers were like him, we'd never lose any wars. In the second round, we both moved in to throw shots and clashed heads.

I knew it was a bad cut from the look on Ryan's face. When he told me I was 'absolutely fine', that made things even worse. In boxing, 'you're absolutely fine' usually translates as 'you're fucked, mate'.

When the ref wandered over, he said the cut was caused by a punch, so I was thinking: 'Here we go; they're trying to stiff me again.' But Ryan told me to just box and stay away from him, which I managed to do. I also put him down with a body shot in the fifth and ended up winning comfortably on points. But it was a tough gig, like all my fights were tough gigs (apart from against Sandor Horvath). I'd ended up involved in a bloodbath and on the verge of being stopped on a technical decision. Some way to ease myself back in.

Not long after beating Van Poetsch, Dave gave me a call.

'Right, I've got a fight for you.'

'Who against?'

'Arek Malek. He's had almost 80 fights and lost most of them.'

'What do I want to fight him for?'

'Because when you beat him, you'll fight for the British title.'

'Fuck off.'

'I promise you. I've done the deal.'

I was speechless. I started welling up. Dave didn't have to ask if I wanted the fight and didn't have to mention money; he just told me it was happening. I think he was almost as emotional as me. That must have been a great phone call to make: telling his fighter he'd finally made his dream come true.

Eddie Hearn had just signed Darren Hamilton and was looking for a fall guy. Darren needed to defend the British light-welterweight title one more time to win the Lonsdale Belt outright and I'd been roped in to add a few more column inches, show up, put up a decent fight and lose. Eddie saw the match as a great addition to his show, and the fact that he was good friends with Dave, and Dave was good friends with Darren's manager Spencer Fearon, smoothed the fight's passage. But if it hadn't been for Luke Campbell, it still probably wouldn't have happened, because Eddie wouldn't have been staging shows in Hull. As it was, Luke was contesting his fifth pro fight at the Ice Arena and the fact I was a local fighter was the final piece of the puzzle. That bit of luck I'd been looking for came when I needed it most. The stars had finally aligned.

Because my previous fight had been at welterweight, I had to drop back down to get ranked at light-welterweight, hence the fight with Malek. Even though it was only a six-round tune-up, I was really worried. I'd just had life-or-death with Van Poetsch and was still utterly convinced I could lose to anyone. But I boxed clever, kept it long, didn't try to knock him out, and outpointed him easily. Conveniently, I suddenly appeared at number 10 in the light-welterweight rankings, which meant that Hamilton was allowed to pick me as a voluntary opponent. Bingo.

One problem remained: namely, that the British Boxing Board of Control wasn't keen on the match at all. I'd been inserted in the top 10, I'd won the English title, I'd fought an eliminator, I'd lost on a split decision to the current British and Commonwealth champion in the weight above, and the men in blazers still didn't want me in their club. Despite all the evidence to the contrary, they still found it difficult to believe a footballer was worthy of boxing for their most prestigious belt: 'What happens if he wins? Have we then got to say he's good?'

Sense prevailed. In the end they voted on whether or not to sanction the fight and, although the panel was split 3-2, it was waved through. And once they'd waved it through, I was doubly determined to prove them wrong. There's nothing like being barred from a club to make you desperate to join it.

People think you get paid handsomely for a shot at the British title. I was offered 10 grand. Eddie Hearn is a smarmy bastard. When he appears on TV with that smug little grin on his face, I can see how he winds people up. But as well as making me chuckle, he's a decent bloke. He gave me my big chance and always paid me on time. That said, his monopoly on Sky is not good for the British boxer. If Eddie phones me up and offers me 10 grand to fight for the British title, I either agree to it or I don't fight – there's no wriggle room. I don't blame Eddie – it's business – but he had me by the bollocks.

Promoters also know the boxers who just love to fight, and I was one of them. If someone walked into a pub and insulted me, I'd iron him out, no qualms. I fought Billy Smith for 500 quid, and after I'd paid my trainer I came out with 450. I spent it all in a lap-dancing club straight afterwards. So Eddie knew I'd have fought Darren Hamilton for peanuts. If Floyd Mayweather is the 'Money Man', I was the 'Money Means Nothing Man'. Just let me at 'em.

CHAPTER 32

I'D RATHER BE DEAD

I always told Dave that if he got me the British title fight, I wouldn't lose. Because I couldn't. There's a massive difference between wanting to win and having to win. I was killing myself to make 10 stone, I was 33, I'd already lost six times, my body was falling apart, I had maybe six months left in the game and my shot had almost been vetoed by the Board of Control. Unless I got robbed and there was a clamour for a rematch, this was the last chance saloon. And if we fought second time around, Darren Hamilton would know my game plan and train like a lunatic. I felt intense pressure. The promise that had been nagging away at me became a foghorn in my ear. All I could think about – when I was lying in bed, when I was out on the road, when I was banging away at the heavy bag – was what might happen if I didn't do what I had to. What would I say? How would I feel? But I knew if I didn't do it, it would destroy my life.

This was some predicament I'd got me and my family into. For Charlotte, it must have been frightening to live with. She knew the consequences if it didn't happen and she knew I was willing to die in the ring to make it happen. I was being stalked, day and night, by a chilling thought: 'If I don't pull this off, I'd rather be dead.'

Thankfully, I managed to assemble a dream team of people who understood exactly what it meant to me. Adam Booth knew me from my time at Hayemaker Promotions, so when the fight was rubber-stamped he phoned Dave and asked if there was anything he could do to help in terms of sponsorship or training money. When Dave called to tell me, I said: 'To be honest, the best thing Adam could give is his time. That would be so much more valuable than bunging me five grand.' Dave phoned back half an hour later and said: 'Can you start Monday?' Adam cleared eight weeks of his diary for me and training with him was worth a million pounds. Adam is like Marmite – I hear a lot of people saying negative things about him. But he'd been there, seen it and done it with David Haye, guiding him to cruiserweight and heavyweight world titles. He reminded me of Yoda – the force is strong with Adam. When he speaks about boxing, my advice is to listen because he knows his shit.

I'd never gone into that much detail before; he dissected everything. I just used to throw punches, but he taught me different ways to throw them. For example, he taught me how to throw my jab so that it would negate my opponent's jab. He also got me in incredible shape. Because of the operations I'd had on my knee, I couldn't do all the roadwork I wanted to. But Adam still had me doing these outrageous track sessions. I'd have to do 10 lots of 800m, and after every 800m he'd say to me: 'Nine rounds to go, go again ... eight rounds to go, go again ...' Before the last few, my legs would be like fag ash, but he'd say to me: 'You're two rounds down with three to go, go again ...'

In my head, I'd have to beat my previous times to win the British title. And I always managed it. I was also sparring world-class boxers and doing well. Andy Lee was on the verge of winning a world middleweight title, while Nathan Cleverly had only recently lost his world light-heavyweight belt. Adam would say to me: 'You're sparring Andy Lee here. He's miles bigger and better than Darren Hamilton and you're holding your own.' Andy would switch to orthodox to replicate Hamilton's awkward, erky-jerky style, but he'd also cut loose and hurt me. Ryan Rhodes remained a key part of my team – I was in London four days a week with Adam but in Rotherham three days a week with Ryan – as was former British welterweight title challenger Gary Logan. After sparring, I'd wrestle with judo guru Bobby Rich, to really sap my energy. Being surrounded by an elite team bolstered my confidence. After a while, I felt like I belonged. Everything had aligned again: 'I'm ready for this. Fuck everyone.'

That was a boring Christmas. No booze, no partying, no nothing. I'd sometimes balloon up to 13 stone between fights and have to take all that weight off, but this time I went no heavier than 11 and a half. People talked about how tough and fit Darren Hamilton was, but I knew I was fitter and tougher. More importantly, I knew I wanted it more. He'd been like me once, had come from nowhere and climbed to the top of the mountain to win his British title against all odds. But once you've made it and have planted your flag in the soil, you're never the same again. He could tell me as many times as he liked how desperately he wanted to hang on to his Lonsdale Belt and win it outright, but I knew I was hungrier. Since he'd been signed by Eddie Hearn, he'd become full of himself and slacked off. If that fight had taken place 12 months earlier he would have trained like a demon. But now he was taking opponents lightly and I was convinced that arrogance would be his undoing.

It wasn't just about drawing him into a dogfight; the plan was more scientific than that. I knew that all he had was his awkwardness and his jab. If I could take his jab away from him, I knew I could beat him. The first time I came face to face with him I was surprised by how big he was. But I've got long arms and my reach was longer than that of most of my opponents, including Hamilton. So I knew that if I got my timing right I could outjab him, which would be the last thing he was expecting. If you're a puncher and you get in the ring with someone who hits harder, it messes with your mind. Similarly, if you're a boxer and you get in the ring with an opponent who starts outjabbing you, you immediately think: 'Bollocks. How's he outjabbing me? He's shit!'

I got on well with everyone I fought, apart from Shayne Singleton and Darren Hamilton. My beef with Hamilton had a lot to do with his manager Spencer Fearon, who was the mouth of the south. But I genuinely disliked Darren. I didn't like the way he spoke to me, how he tried to belittle me and discredit anything I'd done. He thought I was shit, was lucky to get my shot, and he told me so. And that was perfect for me. Just like those days on Northfield Crescent, Darren's words lit a fire under me and sharpened my edges. If you're going to have a do-or-die fight with someone, thinking they're a prick helps.

Darren was constantly telling me how 'gangster' he was and even recorded a rap about me, which was hilarious. Bear in mind he was a black guy from down south, so all that gangster stuff was going down like a shit sandwich with the locals. Because he'd been living rough before he won the British title, he seemed to think that made him tougher than me. But I told him: 'If I had nowhere to stay, I'd just ring one of my mates and they'd let me sleep on the sofa. You must be some kind of wanker if nobody wants to help you out.' We nearly came to blows at one of the press conferences, I really wanted to do him, and there was more argy-bargy at the weigh-in. The face-off lasted about a minute and we were actually touching noses for most of it. He kept shouting at me: 'Where are your tactics? How are you going to beat me?!' I knew I was going to outbox him but I kept on saying: 'Stand and fight and I'll knock you out.' The best game plan is to convince your opponent you have no game plan. I'd been working for eight weeks on how to outbox him and he thought I only had a puncher's chance. I was five steps ahead of him, the silly bastard.

CHAPTER 33

FREE AT LAST

Hull, February 2014

I barely slept the night before the fight. The Ice Arena was only a few miles from where I lived but I stayed in a hotel away from the wife and kids. I wanted to be alone, so that I could focus fully on what it meant to me. I convinced myself I was going to stop him with a right uppercut followed by a left hook to the body, because I'd put a couple of people down with that shot in sparring. But I didn't dwell on tactics; I tried to build the emotion instead. Part of me didn't want the day to come. Dreams are sometimes better left as dreams, because reality is far more frightening. When I woke up, I remember thinking: 'Oh fuck ...' Doomsday was approaching – events that would determine the rest of my life.

Adam and the team arrived at the hotel on Saturday morning and that day was the longest of my life. Longer than all those days on Northfield Crescent, waiting for a bomb to go off; longer than all those days spent in police cells; longer than all those days sat on my sofa in Birmingham, feeling ashamed and drinking myself into oblivion. We went for a walk and Dave said to me: 'If you were fighting Darren Hamilton at the Magna, not on the telly and not for the British title, what do you think would happen?'

'I'd beat him easy.'

'You would, wouldn't you? He wouldn't live with you. That's the way you've got to treat it – as just another fight.'

It's great saying that, and it gets said in sport all the time, but the reality was different. It wasn't just another fight; it was my whole life on the line.

I always liked to wallow in fear in the dressing room before a fight. I never had any music, because music took my mind off the job. I wasn't there to have a good time – I was there to fight. I was a kill-or-be-killed type of fighter. I was never going to completely outbox someone, so I didn't need to get loose as a goose and be dancing around like Naseem Hamed. I needed to be scared and on edge: 'You're going to get hurt tonight, but you're going to get through it.' Adam was used to fighters loosening themselves up with loud music and everyone having a good time, and here I was sitting in the corner, rocking backwards and forwards. He was probably thinking: 'Is this kid all right? It looks like he's having a breakdown.' It was eerie, like being in the trenches again, waiting for someone to blow the whistle. I was right on the edge, getting choked up because of the enormity of the situation: 'Just get me in there and let the punches fly.'

Adam was a master tactician but also a great psychologist. For whatever reason, he understood my anxiety, knew what was going on inside my head: 'Jesus Christ, what's gonna happen if I don't do this? Everything's gonna fall apart.' As we were walking to the ring, to the strains of 'My Way', he tapped me on the shoulder and said: 'You know this fight means nothing in the grand scheme of things?' Suddenly all the tension lifted and my head cleared. I went from being right on the edge and wanting to knock Darren Hamilton's head off to thinking: 'Yeah, he's right. Just getting to this point has been a massive achievement. Hardly anyone expects you to win; you're a big underdog with the pundits and the bookies. So don't think about winning, just enjoy it. Do what you've been doing for the last eight weeks and you'll walk away a happy man.'

I couldn't have dreamed up the scenario any better. I was fighting round the corner from Dad's old pub and just about everyone I knew was there. It was perfect. The place was like a bear pit – the crowd was singing my name and going nuts. I'd convinced myself that everyone wanted me to fail and only at that moment did I realise how much my dream meant to other people. It was like emerging from some dark tunnel, covered in shit, and seeing thousands of people lining the streets applauding. All the time I'd been crawling through that tunnel I thought I was alone, but it wasn't true. When Darren came out wearing a top hat, with some rapper next to him, the hostility was breathtaking – he was being called every name under the sun. Back in the 1980s, Hull was a National Front hotbed, so I was licking my lips: 'There'll be a fair few people hating this – you've already lost two rounds. Still feeling tough? Welcome to my house.'

Before the first bell, we were both crouched like sprinters. When it sounded, we burst out of our blocks. But we were kidding each other. Darren was an awkward bastard and it was difficult to get close in the early rounds, which meant it was far more technical than many people expected. But I soon worked out that his jab was more of a frustration than an offensive weapon, so I was able to walk through it without getting hurt. By the third I was outjabbing him and getting through to the body. The top half of his body was massive but his legs were like matchsticks, so part of the plan was to go to the body early and bury him down the stretch if I had to. He'd expected me to come out like a caveman but I was matching him technically and had his respect. I could hear Adam in the corner shouting, 'Make him miss!', over and over again. And I did, repeatedly. By the fifth round he was the one getting frustrated and I had his corner worried. He showed a bit more urgency in the sixth, landing with a couple of right uppercuts and pinning me on the ropes. But he used up a lot of energy with those attacks and I was back at it the following round.

The fight caught fire at the end of the eighth. I landed with a left hook followed by a right cross and he hit back with an overhand right. By now the crowd was going ballistic – that was the only time I can remember the hairs on the back of my neck standing up while I was actually fighting. After the ninth, Adam said to me: 'You know this is close? You've got to win 10, 11 and 12 to achieve everything you ever wanted.' Two rounds down with three to go. I'd been here before without even knowing it: pounding the track, legs like fag ash. I always managed it then, so why not now? I put everything into those last three rounds. It was the culmination of all that abuse on Northfield Crescent, added to all that shame about my football career, added to wanting to prove so many people wrong, added to wanting to do it for so many people, added to an all-consuming fear of what might happen if I came up short. Every punch I threw was to hammer home a promise to a stubborn kind of fellow I once knew.

I knew I could outlast him because of all the training I'd done, and not just in the previous eight weeks. Doing twice as much work as everyone else for almost a decade was paying dividends when it mattered most. And as I'd predicted, he didn't want it as much as I did, even if only subconsciously. Not many people who climb Everest go back and climb it again. Once you've climbed it, you've climbed it. Darren knew what the view looked like from up there and was getting bored of it. I'd never been up there. I'd made it halfway a few times but kept getting chucked back down. So now I was nearly at the top, I wasn't going to lose my footing. I hurt him in the 10th but he upped his pace in the 11th and caught me with a wicked uppercut. But I came on strong in the 12th, wobbling him with a couple of overhand rights, and even thought I might stop him. By now, everyone was on their feet and I could hear the chant: 'C-U-R-T-I-S! C-U-R-T-I-S!' Every time I landed – even when I nearly landed – the place erupted. The fans were doing everything in their power to shove me across the line: 'He's gonna do this! Get over, yer bastard!'

I'd been in harder fights. The last few rounds were a bit

of a tear-up, but physically it wasn't particularly draining, because it wasn't fast-paced and he had no power. But when I heard the final bell, I suddenly felt shattered. It was like I'd been hollowed out inside, emptied of any emotion. Ross Burkinshaw, who was also part of the team, was first into the ring, hugging me and screaming in my ear: 'You're the British champ! You're the British champ!' When the rest jumped in, they were all saying the same, while David Haye and Kell Brook were going nuts ringside. I thought I'd won – and from Darren's initial reaction, he thought I'd won – but I wasn't doing any cartwheels. Even seeing Eddie Hearn's face, which looked like a smacked arse, didn't reassure me. When it's you in the fight, it's sometimes difficult to judge whether you've done enough or not. And I'd been here before, against Jay Morris, Peter McDonagh, Frankie Gavin and Shayne Singleton. 'Sorry, pal, nice effort, especially for a footballer, but we're still not letting you into our club ...'

When me and Dave went for our walk on the morning of the fight, he'd said to me: 'Imagine if you're stood there, it's gone to points and they announce it's a split decision. What would you do?'

'I'd shit myself. That would just about sum it all up.'

Sure enough, a split decision was what it was. As against Singleton and as against Gavin. When the MC made the announcement, I turned to look at Dave and shrugged my shoulders, as if to say: 'I can't fucking believe this ...' I started praying, to who I don't know: 'Somebody – anybody! Help me ...'

'... *Judge Michael Alexander scores the contest ... 116-113, in favour of Hamilton ...*'

'... Please don't fuck me this time, I've been through too much shit for you to fuck me ...'

'... *Steve Gray scores the contest ... 116-115, in favour of Woodhouse ...*'

'... Please, please, please just give me this one. I don't want anything else. I know I've won it, everyone knows I won it, just give me this one ...'

'... *And finally ... judge Marcus McDonnell scores the contest ... 116-114 ... in favour of ... a-a-a-a-a-nd THE NEW ...*'

I didn't hear anything else. I don't believe in God and I don't believe in heaven but I do believe someone was looking out for me: 'Listen, you've been through enough, you've earned your stripes, come on in.' The place went mental – there was a ring full of shiny, happy people. Crying, roaring, screaming. I wish I could have bottled that feeling and kept it forever. My first goal for Sheffield United, the births of my three kids, my wedding day – none of that came close. I can hear Charlotte now: 'You can't say that!' Sorry, love, I just did.

Dave jumped like a flea into my arms and we both started blubbing like a couple of schoolgirls. For him, as much as me, it was mission impossible accomplished. When I was getting beat, we were getting beaten together. But he kept the faith and it's always better when you go on a hard, long slog with other people, because when you reach the goal, you get to share the satisfaction. Adam had trained a heavyweight world champion but that night was just as special for him, because he saw how much it meant to me. Eddie Hearn obviously wasn't over the moon, his fighter had just lost, but even he seemed genuinely pleased for me. When he shook my hand he just said: 'Fucking unbelievable.'

As expected, arrogance lost Darren that fight. He was a better boxer and I could have boxed a hell of a lot better; the tension got the better of me. But I did a number on him mentally, which made it even sweeter. He must have been sat in his dressing room afterwards, thinking: 'How did I just lose to Curtis Woodhouse?' But he was gracious in defeat, told me I'd earned his respect. Even though I'd taken his title, deep down he must have been happy for me, because he'd crawled through an awful lot of shit himself.

In my post-fight interview, I dedicated the win to Dad and broke down again. Dave and Ryan soon followed suit. Most people watching probably thought I was always like that, blubbing at the drop of a hat, but I hadn't cried for about 20 years. It was all just so raw. I also said I was going to retire, and I meant it. It was similar to how I'd felt after my last game of professional football, the playoff final for Grimsby: I knew instantly that I didn't want to fight again. 'Thank fuck that's over. Exclamation mark. Full stop.' I'd done it. How could I ever top what happened that night? Most importantly, I'd fulfilled my promise.

The first thing I did when I got back to my dressing room was phone the kids. Charlotte's mum put Kyle, who was 10 at the time, on the phone: 'I've done it, mate. I'm the British champion!'

'I know, Dad, we were watching on TV!'

'I told you you weren't allowed to watch it!'

'I know. But we wanted to see you win. You all right, Dad?'

'Yeah, I'm all right mate. I'll see you in the morning.'

I had him on loudspeaker and, when I hung up, all these former boxers, proper hard bastards – Ryan Rhodes, Dave Coldwell, Gary Logan – were pretending they had something in their eyes. That must have been a very dusty dressing room. And Kyle had a superhero, at least for one night.

Everyone was after their pound of flesh and it was nice that people wanted to slap me on the back and congratulate me. But I'd known plenty of Johnnies-come-lately in football and only wanted to be with people who'd been by my side throughout my boxing odyssey. That was the best part of it, seeing what it meant to everyone else. But the euphoria quickly started to fade. Even in the dressing room, I was thinking to myself: 'You'll never get that feeling again. It's gone forever.' But there was one thing they could never take away from me: 'Curtis Woodhouse, British champion.' That was me from now on.

I took my belt to a bar down the road and it seemed like everyone I'd ever met was in there. But I had one bottle of lager and left. I'd done all that stuff in football – the after-parties, drinking champagne in VIP suites, the glitz and glamour, people falling into my fists – and ruined most of the good moments I'd had. I used to get so pissed I'd forget why I was celebrating in the first place: 'What about that goal!'

'What happened again? I can't really remember . . .'

I didn't want to get drunk and forget my greatest moment; I wanted to soak it all in, remember every minute of it. So me and Charlotte shuffled off into the night. When we left, we couldn't find a cab. So there I was, the new British champion, Lonsdale Belt over my shoulder, kicking my heels on the streets of Hull. Luckily, one of the guys who worked on the show pulled over.

'Hello, mate. Have you just won the British title?'

'Yeah, that's me.'

'What you doing standing here?'

'Trying to get a cab home.'

'Jump in, I'll give you a lift.'

So now it's me, Charlotte and the Lonsdale Belt huddled in the back of this geezer's van, with all his work gear falling over us. He dropped us off at a kebab house. Charlotte ordered a chicken kebab, I bought chicken and chips, and we took the takeaway back to our hotel room. Not exactly *Rocky* – 'Yo Adrian! I did it!' – more like: 'Well done, love. Are you finished with those chips?' We watched a bit of telly and were in bed by 11.30. But it was the perfect end to the perfect day. It was important I spent my crowning moment with the person who meant most to me, and not with some pissed-up geezer in a bar telling me he always knew I'd do it.

Without Charlotte, none of it would have happened. I dragged her and the kids through a lot of shit, but she never wavered in her support. Not even when I was off the rails and she was probably thinking: 'I've got kids, I could do without this.' And not even when I was all bashed up and she must have wondered if she'd be pushing me around in a wheelchair one day. If you'd watched my fights on TV, you wouldn't have seen her. She wasn't one of those partners who got all dolled up and sat ringside, screaming her head off. But she was always there, back in the cheap seats, making sure I got home safely. And when I didn't make it home safely, she was there by my hospital bed. We finally tied the knot in 2013, 11 years after we first met, but I never had any doubts. From the iceberg that sank the *Titanic*, Charlotte ended up being my lucky charm.

I knew my window of glory wouldn't last that long, so I planned to enjoy it. But this time I did it the right way. Charlotte's mum brought the kids to the hotel so that I could show them the belt and we had a nice breakfast. Darren's manager, Spencer Fearon, popped over and told me how proud Dad would have been of me, which he didn't have to do. And when other people stopped to tell me what an amazing achievement it was, this time I was able to remember what they were referring to. Not that I didn't have a few drinks later. Pretty much everyone who'd been at the fight met at Mum's pub in Driffield and the place was absolutely rammed. When the replay came on the telly, everyone watched it as if it was live. I was standing at the bar with the belt over my shoulder, not really looking at the screen. Instead, I was watching all these people roaring and screaming, and thinking: 'I don't want to spoil it for anyone, but I win!' Beer was flying everywhere, people were telling me their stories of the night, and that just meant the world to me. It was validation: 'You're not a fuck-up. You've made amends, achieved something great. You've done what you set out to do and nobody can ever say you didn't. No more "buts". Now you can sleep easy.'

But before the party I paid a couple of important visits. First, I called in on Nana, the amazing lady who made it all possible. Towards the end of her life Nana had Alzheimer's and wasn't too sure who anybody was. But when I showed her the write-ups of the fight in the newspapers, for a brief moment she understood. When she told me how proud she was, that was poignant. The next visit was to Dad's grave. As soon as I woke up, I knew that's what I wanted to do. When I was older, and I realised he might not actually live forever, Dad used to say to me: 'I hope I don't go to heaven – I won't know anyone there.' I don't believe in heaven and I don't know where he is. But I still felt the need to say thank you. I laid my belt on the headstone he shares with his brother Carson and breathed a huge sigh of relief. 'There you go, Dad. I promised you I'd do it.' Suddenly I felt completely peaceful. When I left that graveyard, I was a different person to the man who'd walked in. I didn't need to worry anymore; I could get on with the rest of my life without being haunted by this horrible 'what if'. There would be no more waking up in a cold sweat and thinking: 'Why did I make that promise? I can't keep it. I'm not going to do this. What's going to happen to me and my family?' I was free at last.

CHAPTER 34

A LITTLE BIT SICK

You didn't seriously think there would be a fairy-tale ending? This is boxing, not Disney. People ask me all the time why I boxed on. I boxed on for the same reason almost every fighter boxes on when everyone else wants him to quit: I needed the money. Becoming a professional fighter probably cost me £1m. Everything I'd earned as a footballer had been ploughed back into this dream and now I was skint. On my way to the weigh-in for the Hamilton fight, I got a call from the taxman, who informed me I had an unpaid bill for 70-odd grand. I said I wasn't going to pay it, so they made me bankrupt. Before the Hamilton fight, I'd told everyone I'd collect 250 grand on a bet if I won the British title. So at my meeting with the taxman, he kept asking me where the money was. I told him it was none of his business: 'It could be buried in my garden. But it might not be. Good luck trying to find it.' I was just messing with him. Even now, I will neither confirm nor deny whether I won that money or not.

When I texted Dave to tell him I was carrying on, he thought I was joking. He begged me not to and, when I insisted, he announced that he wanted nothing to do with it and handed back my contract. The conversation with Charlotte wasn't easy either. But while she wasn't happy, she also knew I didn't really have a choice. It's all very well people wanting a Hollywood ending and for me to walk into the sunset with a smile on my face and a big bag of swag over my shoulder, but that wasn't the reality. I could have fought for the European title against Italy's Michele Di Rocco but Adam Booth advised me against it: 'This guy will be punching and moving – he's the worst possible match for you. Unless they're offering you ridiculous amounts of money, don't do it.' They weren't, so I didn't. But I was offered 35 grand to put my British title on the line against Commonwealth champion Willie Limond. My previous highest purse had been 14 grand for fighting Frankie Gavin. I got 10 grand for the Hamilton fight, eight grand for fighting Derry Mathews, four grand for the blood bath against Dave Ryan. And for most of my career, I was on £2,500 a fight. Deep down I knew I was done, but I had to go again. From pulling off a story you couldn't make up, I'd suddenly become a boxing cliché.

My pride wouldn't allow me to come out and say I needed the money, just as no boxer ever says he needs the money. Most people assumed I was a millionaire and I was fine with that. So I trotted out all the old lines. About still improving as a boxer, about still having so much to give, about wanting to leave a legacy. Meanwhile, I was hating every minute of training. I'd conquered my Everest and was already bored of the view. I was taking more and more punches to the head in sparring; I was getting more and more headaches. My knees were completely shot, my back went four weeks before the fight and I couldn't train for a fortnight, which made making weight an even more excruciating ordeal than usual. The British Boxing Board of Control says you're not allowed to use saunas to lose weight, but I had to because I could no longer make weight healthily or legally. And all the while, I knew I was fighting someone who was far better than me. Limond had been in with Amir Khan and Mexican legend Erik Morales, had lost two British title challenges against Alex Arthur and Anthony Crolla. He was a bit too clever, a bit too sharp, a bit too everything.

I knew I was on the slide before the Hamilton fight, but at least I had the carrot of winning the British title. Now, that incentive was gone. Dave had a great analogy: It's like when you've just eaten a great meal, the best you've ever had, and you sit back and think: 'That was awesome.' Then, the waiter comes over and says: 'Sir, would you like to see the dessert menu?' You don't really want to, because you're already satisfied. But you have a look anyway. Next minute, you've got a half-eaten trifle in front of you and you feel fat as anything, a little bit sick, wishing you hadn't bothered.

Glasgow, June 2014

I woke up on the morning of the weigh-in seven pounds over the 10st light-welterweight limit. I was close to tears, sitting on my bed in the hotel room. Ryan Rhodes and my good mate Sharky were with me. If I didn't make the weight, the fight was off and I wouldn't get paid. So I had to sweat it off in a hot bath. Ryan had to lift me out and, when my feet made contact with the floor, my legs gave way and I fainted. When I got out of the cold bath Ryan had run to bring me round, I suddenly felt really light-headed. Then I had to go to the weigh-in and pretend I felt great. Amazingly, I made weight at the first time of asking and, from being a wreck a couple of hours earlier, I was now buzzing.

The buzz didn't last long. The dressing room before the fight was like a morgue. I'd always liked a spooky atmosphere, but this was different. Afterwards, my best mate Wardy said: 'You couldn't pay me to go in your dressing room again – it was like sitting with someone about to go to the electric chair. I was shitting myself and I wasn't even fighting.' Before the Hamilton fight, I was the one who needed to win. This time, it was Limond who needed it, because he'd never won the British title before and a defeat would probably have ended his career. Despite the injuries, I trained hard for that fight, but I lacked any kind of edge. And, despite the bout taking place in Limond's hometown of Glasgow, there was no atmosphere; it was a bit of a damp squib. I'd have preferred it if everyone was chucking beer bottles at me – at least it might have wound me up: 'Fuck everyone.' But I'm not even sure that would have worked.

Limond put me down with a left uppercut in the third and again with a right uppercut in the 11th. I got up both times because, though I didn't need to win, I still wanted to and had my pride. He didn't manage to get me out of there before the final bell but he fully deserved the victory. In the dressing room afterwards, I felt strangely relieved that I hadn't won, just like I'd felt strangely relieved that I hadn't won the playoff final with Grimsby. If I'd beaten Limond, I would have been tempted to go again, because I would probably have got paid even more. I'd have been in the same situation I was in at Rushden & Diamonds, competing purely for the money, going through the motions like a zombie.

My face was a mess; I needed 10 stitches and both eyes had gone. The boss of the Board of Control, Robert Smith, popped into the dressing room and said: 'You've had a great career; have a long, hard think about what you're going to do now.' Charlotte, Mum, Ryan, Dave, Wardy – everyone wanted me to retire. You rarely get perfect endings in boxing, but I'd lost my title how I wanted to: I'd given my all and been beaten by a better man. Nobody ever mentions that fight, because it wasn't important.

A couple of months after the Limond fight, I received a special recognition prize at the British Boxing Board of Control Awards. That night was every bit as special as winning the British title. I received a standing ovation and, when I looked around the room, I could see a host of legends of the fight game, all clapping away with enormous smiles on their faces: Nigel Benn, Chris Eubank, Lloyd Honeyghan, Frank Bruno, Joe Calzaghe, Anthony Joshua – the list goes on. They must have been thinking: 'How the hell did he manage that? He must be mental, but what a story!' I just felt like crying. I don't give a shit whether or not a bloke in a bar or on Twitter thinks I'm a great boxer, but to be acknowledged for what I'd achieved by my fellow fighters was a really humbling experience. I don't think I'll ever really feel like one of them; I'll always be the footballer-turned-boxer. But some very good fighters never won a British title. Unlike all these other bullshit titles you have nowadays – 'silver' titles, 'masters' titles, 'international' titles – which you can win in a packet of cornflakes, they don't give British titles away.

A lot of fighters dodge the British title and take an easier route, because they're not good enough. But I'd done it and no one could say I hadn't. When I see the list of British light-welterweight champions, my name sticks out like a sore thumb. In years to come, people will scan that list and read all those names – Junior Witter, Ricky Hatton, Terry Marsh, Clinton McKenzie, Dave 'Boy' Green – and then they'll come to mine: 'Curtis Woodhouse? Wasn't he a footballer?' And they'd be right. But I could box a bit as well.

The problem was, proving people wrong had become an obsession. So now everyone was telling me to retire, it didn't sit well with me. Dave and Ryan would say: 'You're done now; you're getting hurt by people who shouldn't be hurting you. You're only going to go one way.' Deep down inside, I knew they were right, but I didn't like hearing it. It pissed me off. It was me who'd crawled through all that shit to get to where I had, so I was going to bow out when I wanted to bow out, and not when anyone else wanted me to. I'd spent my entire sporting career, from when I was that skinny little kid on Northfield Crescent, being told what I couldn't do. So now that people were telling me I didn't have it anymore, my natural reaction was: 'I've been proving people wrong for 25 years; I've still got a couple of years left in me.' I wasn't willing to accept that suddenly they were right about me. I was fighting on. Fuck everyone.

So I agreed on a three-year managerial deal with Dennis Hobson, who had guided Clinton Woods and Stuart Hall to world titles, and trotted out all the old lines again. About still improving as a boxer, about still having so much to give, about wanting to leave a legacy. Then I started to train. Or, rather, I didn't. I did a couple of runs and my knee kept blowing up. Dennis suggested I have a good spar, to get the hunger back and assess my fitness, but I kept putting it off: 'Oh, I can't really come in today; I've got to go shopping with the missus and drop the kids off.' Suddenly, everything seemed more important than boxing. I'd ticked the box and lost interest. The thought of getting punched in the head no longer seemed so appealing. In the end, I was pretending to train because I couldn't bear admitting to people that they'd been right and I'd been wrong. And then boxing had one of those terrible nights that made up my mind for me.

I'd sparred more rounds with Jerome Wilson than any other fighter and we appeared on quite a few shows together at the Magna in Rotherham. Jerome was a very talented boxer from Sheffield, miles better than I was. He was fast, elusive, hit hard, and we knocked a lot of lumps out of each other down the years. The difference was that I could afford to be a full-time boxer, because of my football money, but he could only afford to box part time because of his other commitments. On 12 September 2014, I was co-commentating on his rematch with Serge Ambomo, on a Dave Coldwell show in Sheffield. Jerome went down in the second round and again in the sixth, this time more heavily. I'll never forget the look on his mum's face as he lay motionless on the canvas.

I put down my microphone and went to see if he was all right. A journalist from the Sheffield *Star* was filming on his mobile phone, from about a metre away, as Jerome fought for his life. That made me feel sick. I said to him: 'What the fuck are you doing? This is serious – you could be filming the last moments of his life.' He started going on about his responsibility as a journalist. He couldn't care less about the kid on the deck; he just wanted the hits.

Jerome's family, including his wife and daughter, left with him as he was rushed to hospital on a stretcher. They were told it was touch and go and that he might not make it through the night. Jerome had a bleed on the brain and was in a coma for 10 days. He eventually made a good recovery, but witnessing that happen to somebody in such tremendous physical condition, who was twice as good as me at boxing and five years younger, really shook me. How could I put myself back into that situation, with my mum, my wife and everyone else sat watching? I'm selfish, but that would be pushing it too far and be unfair to so many people. I always thought something bad was going to happen to me anyway, and Jerome's terrible injury would have made my pre-fight anxiety even worse. So I weighed it all up and decided I wasn't going to risk it. Everyone had been right and I'd been wrong. Just leave it there, mate. And that was that. I never even phoned Dennis Hobson. We both just pretended it never happened.

CHAPTER 35

MY WAY

I don't know if you've ever seen the film *Goodfellas*, but just about every sportsperson who's ever retired will be able to relate to the final scene. Ray Liotta is a former gangster who's been rehoused in the suburbs. Just before the credits role, he appears on his doorstep in his dressing gown and picks up a newspaper. And as he looks straight at the camera, you hear his voiceover: 'Today everything's different. There's no action. I'm an average nobody. I get to live the rest of my life like a schnook.'

That was the hardest thing about retiring from sport – going from a life of wild highs and crushing lows to something much more humdrum. One minute that electrical reading on the machine is going berserk, the next it's flatlining. Because I wasn't really a boxer in essence, giving it up didn't affect me in the way it has lots of other fighters. But there's no doubt the sport takes a lot more than it gives, especially if you spend a long time in it. And I couldn't think of anything worse than playing another game of football (unless Russell Slade asked me, obviously). It's the other stuff I miss, especially the unique camaraderie of the gym and all the changing-room nonsense, which is why I'm always on Twitter. I live out in the Yorkshire countryside, in the village of Howden, but Twitter is like a substitute changing room. You can't smear anyone in dubbin on Twitter, or dump them in Sheffield city centre wearing only their pants, but you can still have plenty of banter. I might have to knock Twitter on the head soon, though. Successful managers don't tend to go around winding up fans of other teams.

Reg Holdsworth gave me my first taste of coaching when he was at Lincoln City. I sat on the bench a couple of days a week, enjoyed the experience and thought, 'Maybe this is for me.' At the same time, I realised I'd find it really difficult to be a coach or an assistant manager, because I want to do things my way. In May 2012, I accepted an offer to manage Sheffield FC, the oldest football club in the world. I was excited, but I massively underestimated how much time and effort you have to plough into football management, even at non-league level. The players were part time and the standard wasn't great, but as a manager I was effectively working full time. Players would call to tell me they couldn't train because they were fitting a conservatory or tarmacking a drive and there would be all these other little things going on that I hadn't anticipated.

That same summer I also started training to fight Dave Ryan for the English title, so I was all over the place.

But Sheffield FC was a perfect learning job. A lot of ex-footballers are too proud to manage in non-league; they want to jump straight in at the deep end. But when you jump in at the deep end, you can easily drown. It's like having a title shot in your first fight – you just don't do it. You need to build the foundations, put the fundamentals in place. I learnt so much at Sheffield FC by doing things wrong. And I could do things wrong because there wasn't much pressure on me. Not to sound horrible, but hardly anyone cared.

I left Sheffield at the end of that year because I was edging closer towards the British title and wanted to focus on my boxing 100 per cent (the decision had nothing to do with the straight red I got in my one appearance for the club, after I'd only been on the pitch for six minutes . . .). But the following year, I joined up with Reg Holdsworth again, as his assistant manager at Goole, which is just down the road from Driffield. Reg's problem was that he didn't know many players at that level, so he struggled and got some bad results. The final straw came when our captain, Karl Colley, jumped into the crowd and started swinging haymakers at a fan. I knew Karl from my days at Sheffield United and he wasn't wired up right at the best of times. So an opposition fan calling him a fat bastard when we were losing 3-0 was never going to go down well. Personally, the thing that most embarrassed me was his technique: he threw three punches and missed with all of them. Anyway, Karl was sacked, Reg left a couple of days later and the chairman asked if I could steady the ship until the end of the season. We won something like 10 of our 15 remaining games, but the following season the chairman resigned. I was struggling to get 11 players on the pitch and decided to quit just after Christmas. Again, it was typical non-league bullshit but all part of my apprenticeship – the managerial equivalent of those kickabouts on Northfield Crescent, or being beaten up in the gym by kids who didn't have any hairs on their nuts.

The hardest thing about management was losing. When I was a player and I lost, by the time I got back home it never really crossed my mind again. As a manager, defeat sits with you a lot longer. In those early days, I was questioning every decision I made: 'Should I have done this? What if I'd done that?' All sorts of things were spinning through my head. As a player I was responsible for my own performance; as a manager I'm responsible for 20 lads. And in non-league football, you're not paying them enough money to expect any sort of control over their lives. So you're dealing with players who have been laying bricks or fixing a roof all day. They've had a bacon sandwich for breakfast, a bacon sandwich for lunch, maybe grabbed a bacon sandwich on the way to the game and I'm asking them to run through brick walls for me.

Things are no different at Hull United, the club I joined at the start of 2015. During the 2015/16 season, we got thrown out of two grounds, had to play half of our home games away from home and were deducted 18 points for fielding ineligible players. I was so fed up with the way we were being treated that I resigned for one game, and after I changed my mind the league decided to relegate us. Hull have since secured a 10-year lease at Hull College, which is bang in the middle of the city. They also have a great chairman in Ian Ashbee, who captained Hull City from the old Fourth Division to the Premier League (which he reminds me about at least three times a day), and an ambitious team around him. It's a great project and I think Hull could rise through the leagues, but I was never in it for the long haul. Having earned my UEFA B coaching licence and completed half of the UEFA A course in the summer of 2016, I parted company with Hull and started applying for managerial jobs at Football League clubs. The ultimate goal is landing the top job at Sheffield United. You don't think I've got a hope? I've heard that before, and not just the once.

The fact that I messed up my playing career will be one of my strengths as a manager. I played more than 300 games at every level, from international to Premier League and all the way down to non-league. You might say I did a Jamie Vardy in reverse. I've experienced most things in football and know the game inside out. And that's the beauty of being a massive failure when you're young – it can make you so much wiser when you're older. The key thing I learnt from my playing days, and especially from Russell Slade, was that players play for people, not for the club, and I'm a good people person. I understand what makes people tick and am a good judge of character. I can smell a rat a mile off, because both football and boxing are crawling with them.

I'm not into new-age managing, because football hasn't changed. To be a good manager you need to know the game, be good with people, create a good dressing room and surround yourself with good people who can provide you with information and spot things you haven't seen. Sometimes, when you're in the middle of a forest and all you can see are trees, you need a bit of help. Oh, and it helps if you've got some good players. I'd love to see how Jose Mourinho would get on at Aston Villa. But when I say I'm not into new-age managing, that doesn't mean I'm like Barry Fry. In my admittedly short time in management, I've lost my temper only three or four times. I tap Russell up a lot and he tells me how much he's had to change as a manager. Like Russell, I jot down team talks, to keep them focused and businesslike. Sometimes you need to go mental and throw tea cups around, like Barry, but it doesn't pay to be emotional too often. You've only got about 10 minutes to get your message across, just like a boxing trainer has less than a minute between rounds. So it's better to be cool. I study the game a heck of a lot. But it's not all about tactics and computer analysis; it's about using your eyes and ears. Russell says that being a manager is like being the owner of a bunch of racehorses: your job is to see who's ready to run or who needs putting away for a couple of days. Computers can't tell you whether or not a kid is in the 'danger zone' – just go and ask him how he's feeling. If he wants to play for you, then play him.

I know my way will be successful. But I'll need a chairman or owner to leave me to my own devices. I've already turned down a lot of job offers from Conference teams, because I'm not going to put my head in a noose and be told what to do by someone who doesn't know what they're on about. Too many managers are told which players to buy. But what if I don't want that player? He might be bad for the dressing room, or not fit into my style of play. If you're going to employ someone to cook you a meal, at least let them choose the ingredients. It sounds arrogant, but let me do it my way and I'll get it right.

CHAPTER 36

THE FORMULA

This is the best chapter so far, for me anyway. Out in the sticks with my wife and three kids, it's the happiest I've been in my life. But when I watch my little boy play football, he reminds me of that skinny little kid on Northfield Crescent, head over heels in love with the game. And it makes me want to be a footballer again. I speak to Sheffield United fans now, and for some reason they love me. It makes me feel a little bit ashamed, because I could have given so much more. Writing this book has made me realise that I did achieve a few things in football and did have some happy times, especially those early years at Bramall Lane. I'd just locked them away and never wanted them to come out again. But I still look back and wonder: 'What if?' I try not to think about it too much, though. It's pointless thinking about what I'd do differently if I had my time again, because youth is wasted on the young. Or at least it was wasted on me.

And if I'd fulfilled my promise as a footballer, I'd never have succeeded in boxing. That helps ease the pain. Usually when somebody loses a golden ticket, they don't even bother looking for another one. They wallow in pain rather than searching for salvation. But if a childhood dream evaporates, it's not necessarily the end; it might only be the beginning. Because I'm so single-minded, I never considered how my story might affect other people. But when I won the British title, I was inundated with messages from people telling me how I'd changed their outlook on life. Someone told me they'd finally enrolled for a Spanish course after years of putting it off; someone else told me they'd applied for a job they didn't think they'd get and landed it. I spent my time as British champion well, not like in my football days, when any bit of success was an excuse to get pissed for weeks and shag everything within a 10-mile radius. I gave talks in schools, including the one my little boy and girl went to. They just looked so proud. Hopefully that's a moment they'll remember for the rest of their lives.

Me winning the British title was a little shot in the arm for people. I'm just a scallywag from Driffield, so I found that mind-blowing. But I also understood why. I showed that you can be absolutely useless at something – as Dave Coldwell always reminds me I was – and succeed at it. Not every kid can gain inspiration from David Haye or Joe Calzaghe, because they might not have the same natural talent. But I proved you don't necessarily need that. With enough determination and passion, you can do pretty much anything you want.

People often ask me: 'How the hell did you manage to win the British title?' I'm a dreamer, I suppose. But dreaming isn't enough on its own. If you want to be successful at anything and make your dream a reality, you've got to turn up every single day and work harder than everyone else. Work when you're knackered, work when you're injured, work when there are other things you should be doing, work when people are laughing at you, work for four hours when other people are only working for two. It's not the answer everyone wants to hear, because hard work scares people. I get frustrated by people who don't make the most of what they've got. When Kyle came home from school with a bad report, I went mad and banned him from playing football. If he finds schoolwork difficult, I can live with that. What I can't live with is him not giving 100 per cent.

But it's not just being scared of hard work; it's being scared of failure. There are lots of people out there who have greatness inside them but who will never know it. Someone might be a great singer, but they'll spend the rest of their life singing in the shower if they haven't got the confidence to let others hear them. The only difference between me and them is that I had the balls to roll the dice, an unshakeable conviction. It's about believing in yourself and having the arrogance to say: 'I don't know what it is, but I can be great at something.'

My football career suggested I didn't have the mental strength to succeed in boxing, but I knew it was in there somewhere. I just needed to find it. I'm not thankful for my childhood; it took away a lot more than it gave me. There are things I wish I could erase from my memory which are simply unshakeable. Like most people, my childhood defined the rest of my life. I'm cold and hard and couldn't care less about most people's issues and problems. When I feel cornered, my first impulse is to attack, like a distressed animal. I can feel this terrible rage building inside me, as if I'm a kettle about to explode: heat rising, body shaking, adrenaline pumping, on the brink of tears. For many years, it was uncontrollable. And it was all down to fear. That combination of fear and rage cost me so much. It almost cost me everything.

Maybe it would sound more romantic if I said boxing helped quell the demons inside me. But on reflection, boxing had nothing to do with it. Instead, it was the realisation that none of what happened in my childhood was my fault. For a long time, I thought that if I'd been a better son, Mum and Dad might have stayed together and life would have been sweeter. It took me until my mid-twenties to forgive myself for things that actually had nothing to do with me. I was just a boy of 14 when my mum, brother and sister moved out and left me with a heartbroken superhero. But I don't think I would have achieved the things I did had I not gone through what I went through.

My childhood gave me my resilience and I wish my kids had more of that. My son Kyle is at Rotherham academy and is a good little player. But sometimes I watch him and think: 'He needs a bit of "fuck you" in him.' When I was his age, I'd go round booting people and was always being sent off. He hasn't got that side to him because he's been brought up differently to me. He's loving and caring like his mum and quite emotional. My youngest is more like me; he's got what

Charlotte calls the 'Woodhouse gene'. He's crackers, always wanting to fight and running into things. As for my girl, she takes the piss out of me. A few months ago I bought her a horse, just because she asked for one. Things might change when she starts growing up and bringing home boyfriends, but at the moment it's Kyle and Caleb who bear the brunt of things. But I'll make sure all three of them are nice, polite kids who grow up to be pillars of the community. I wouldn't want any of them to go through what I went through, even if it means they lack my toughness and 'fuck you' attitude.

Luckily, there are easier careers than boxing. If one of my boys came to me and said he wanted to box, I'd do everything in my power to make it not happen. I love boxing, it's one of the best sports out there, but it's for people like me: people who have to fight and people with something to prove. It sounds horrible, but if Dad hadn't died I wouldn't have won the British title because I would have chucked it all in at some point. Sometimes, when I get one of my bad headaches, or my back gives out, or my face goes numb, I wonder if it was all worth it. I think it was. But if not boxing, I reckon it would have been something else.

Retiring from football was the best thing I ever did, I should have done it a lot earlier. Even when you're at school you're programmed to think life is all about money, that you should get your hands on as much as possible. But as soon as you get away from that, you can start doing things that actually make you happy. Some people might think it's weird that punching people and getting punched for not a lot of money made me happy. But it did. I just love fighting. My days of rolling around in nightclubs and car parks are well behind me. But prizefighting is a thing of beauty – you get to peer into another man's soul. Not many people get that opportunity and it's hard to walk away from. So, like a junkie, the urge will always be in me. And I can't promise I'll never use again.

I was worried that football club chairmen and owners might read this book and think I was crazy. I was also worried that Dad might come across as crazy as me, and he's not around to defend himself. He hasn't even got Uncle Carson to back him up, like in the old days. Even when Dad was at his lowest ebb, he never stopped being my superhero. He had his faults but he was fiercely loyal and I could always count on him. He never fell, even when the strongest winds were causing carnage. When Mum left and took Karl and Laura with her, it was just me and him. From that point on, it was us two against the world. I miss him like I could never hope to explain.

I hope I've made it clear that people can change. I believe that I'm now the man I always was deep down. I like life, and life seems to like me. For many years I feared I would always have my own personal black cloud following my every step. But nowadays, when I look up, there are usually blue skies overhead. The demons are still inside but now I'm their master, rather than the other way round. Some of the reasons I'm strict on my boys are the same reasons I'll make a good football manager: I can make out life's pitfalls better than most, because I've fallen into nearly all of them. And I don't like seeing people make the same mistakes as me.

Once you've succeeded at something and thrown it all away, it's actually easier second time around because at least you know the formula for success. I've got it nailed down, because I've succeeded in two sports and also overcome all the bad shit that happened when I was a kid. Players I've managed have wanted to stay with me when they could have moved to teams in higher leagues because they've seen I want the best for them. I'm not exactly that skinny little kid on Northfield Crescent, I've eaten far too many pies for that, but they recognise my determination and passion and the fact that I'm madly in love with football again. We've put our differences behind us, kissed and made up, and now we're looking forward to a bright future together. I even deleted my fight against Darren Hamilton from my TV recordings, as a sort of symbolic divorce. I must have watched that fight a hundred times or more, but cherishing memories too much can stop you from moving forwards. When I started boxing, I wanted to be known as: 'Curtis Woodhouse, former British champion.' But now I am a former British champion, I don't like the sound of it. I don't want to be a 'former' anything. I'm not dead. It's enough that those same players know I made the impossible happen. No former footballer ever won a British title before me, and I don't expect anyone to repeat the feat. Sounds arrogant? Well, you don't get anywhere in life by hiding in your shell.

Once I've managed Sheffield United, I might never manage again. In fact, there's a part of me that never wants to get that job. I might get sacked, like most managers end up doing, and become bitter all over again. But I've got plenty of other things in me – I just don't know what they are yet. While I'm completing my coaching courses, I'm helping to run my tipping website, which is flying. I know it sounds mad, but my job at the moment is watching horse racing and celebrating when the horses win. But I might wake up tomorrow morning and decide I'm bored of it and want to do something else. That's one of the reasons I've put on weight, to make it almost impossible to go back to boxing. Never being satisfied is a gift and a curse, because you never stop chasing the buzz. But it means the highlight might be still to come. I've spoken to Charlotte about climbing Everest. She wouldn't be surprised. But I'd want to climb it quicker than anyone else, just to wind people up. Maybe they'll make a film about me. Who would I get to play Curtis Woodhouse? Me, obviously. Fuck everyone.

I CAN FLY!

I 've been all over the world but Driffield is the place I love best. You might wonder why after what I've told you, but home is home and it made me who I am, for better and for worse. I can walk into any boozer, have a chat and a laugh with old school friends or people I played football with, and they don't give a toss that I played for Sheffield United or won a British title. All the hangers-on and leeches have gone and I know who my real friends are again.

Me and Mum have a great relationship now. She's brilliant with the kids and the first person I ring if I fancy a little Sunday drinking session. When I visited her recently, I combined it with a tour of my old haunts. The shop on the corner, where I used to buy Dad his Walnut Whips and 20 Regals, is gone. But the house on Victoria Road, where I spent so many days and weeks on my own, is still there.

As is Nana's house on Northfield Crescent, although she passed away just after I won the British title. When I looked through the window, I could hear her bossing Dad around: 'Stop doing this, Bernard, do this, Bernard, put that back, Bernard . . .' What a woman – the only person that stubborn old fellow listened to. Our next-door neighbour but one and her Labrador Nigger are long gone, but my first boxing ring is still there – the Brooksby's front garden. I did knock but apparently they didn't fancy a rematch. As for the old pitch where John Barnes used to run the show, I couldn't believe how small it was. And just a concrete circle really. But who needs proper facilities?

Barnes with the tackle . . . Barnes to Beardsley, back to Barnes again . . . Barnes glides past one challenge, and another . . . still Barnes . . . BARNES!

Back at Mum's, we got reminiscing about those times, about the fact that neither she nor Dad discouraged me from believing I could be anything. So when I used to watch John Barnes on the telly, I'd think: 'Why can't I do what he's done?' But Mum also reminded me of something I'd forgotten. When I was small, I was obsessed with Superman. I had the duvet, the pillow, the rug, the curtains, the pyjamas. And when it was time for bed, Mum or Dad would have to carry me upstairs, holding me above their head and singing the Superman theme tune, while I had my fist clenched and arm outstretched. One night, Mum came into my bedroom to find the window wide open and me standing on the ledge.

'Curtis! Come away from the window!'

'It's OK, Mum. I can fly!'

Why wouldn't I be able to fly? I'd seen someone else doing it on the telly and nobody had told me I couldn't.

Dad wasn't the only one in the family who thought he was a superhero. I never really stopped believing I was Superman. Better trying to fly than propping up a bar, telling everyone what you could have been.

ACKNOWLEDGEMENTS

To Mum – tough times don't last, tough people do. We got there in the end. To my little brother, Karl – if I could be anybody else it would be you, a better-looking, kinder version of me! To my little sister, Laura – Dad would have been proud of the young woman and mum you have become. To Charlotte – thanks for your unshakeable devotion to me and our little family. None of it would have been possible without you holding the fort while I was off trying to be Superman. To Kyle, Isla and Caleb – thanks for giving me inspiration to want to do my best. You are the best three things to ever happen to me, nothing comes anywhere close. Daddy loves you always and forever.

To Russell Slade, John Dungworth and Steve Myles – thanks for teaching me everything I know about football. You're the dream team for anybody wanting a career in the beautiful game and inspired me to want to make it. To Gary De'Roux – thanks for starting the fire and giving me your time when most had given up on me. I hope you put that bet on! To Dave Coldwell – thanks for keeping faith when most stopped believing, for building me back up when most wanted to keep me down and hoped I'd fade away. We said we would do it and we did! To Paul Kershaw – that training camp at St Paul's was one of my best, you're destined to be a top trainer of champions. You heard it here first! To Glyn Rhodes – thanks for the pep talk that helped win me the English title. To Les – thanks for the relentless rounds on the body bag, you always got me in fantastic shape. To Jon Pegg – thanks for teaching me how to cut off the ring and making me realise I actually had a jab. And that it wasn't a crime to throw it! To Ryan Rhodes – thanks for being my sparring partner, friend and trainer. It was never easy sharing a ring with the Spice Boy but you were a real inspiration to me and many others. To Adam Booth – you gave me something you can't put a price on, your time. Thanks for sprinkling me with some of your magic dust. To Spencer Fearn – you were the man in the background, the man that nobody saw, but someone who played a massive part in my journey. You're a top bloke, even for a Wednesday fan! To Mark Willie – I'm not sure if I should thank you or not! But whenever you were in the gym I knew I was going to be put through hell and get better as a result. To Owen James – thanks for all your time and effort in getting me into fantastic condition and making sure I was as strong as I could be. I didn't enjoy it but felt the benefits whenever the bell rang.

To Saj at Whitestone Solicitors – you went above and beyond the call of duty as a sponsor. My journey and this book would not have happened without your support, I'm forever in your debt. To Adrian Tolhurst – since our time at school, you've always been somebody to lean on in tough times, whether as a sponsor, gaffer or friend. To Paddy and